Clara Bell, Wilhelmine von Hillern

The Vulture-Maiden

Clara Bell, Wilhelmine von Hillern

The Vulture-Maiden

ISBN/EAN: 9783337017439

Printed in Europe, USA, Canada, Australia, Japan

Cover: Foto ©Thomas Meinert / pixelio.de

More available books at **www.hansebooks.com**

THE
VULTURE MAIDEN

[DIE GEIER-WALLY.]

BY

WILHELMINE von HILLERN.

FROM THE GERMAN
BY
C. BELL and E. F. POYNTER.

Authorized Edition.

L E I P Z I G 1876
B E R N H A R D T A U C H N I T Z.

LONDON: SAMPSON LOW, MARSTON, SEARLE & RIVINGTON.
CROWN BUILDINGS, 188, FLEET STREET.

PARIS: C. REINWALD, 15, RUE DES SAINTS PÈRES; THE GALIGNANI
LIBRARY, 224, RUE DE RIVOLI.

COLLECTION

OF

GERMAN AUTHORS.

VOL. 29.

THE VULTURE MAIDEN BY W. von HILLERN.

IN ONE VOLUME.

TAUCHNITZ EDITION.

By the same Author,

THE HOUR WILL COME . . . . . 2 vols.

CONTENTS.

TO BERTHOLD AUERBACH, Esq.

Permit me to offer you the fruit that I have gathered in a field peculiarly your own. Under your powerful hand the difficult ground of German peasant-life has yielded up its wealth of poetry; and if others, with myself, now reap in the field tilled by you, it is our first duty to think of you with gratitude, and to render to you the honour that is rightly yours.

Freiburg in Brisgau, April 1875.

THE AUTHOR.

mois-hunter, raised his arm threateningly, and pointing her out to the stranger said: "That is certainly
the Vulture-maiden standing up yonder; no other
maid would trust herself on that narrow point, so
near the edge of the precipice.   See, one would
think that the wind must blow her over, but she
always does just the contrary to what other reasonable Christian folk do."

Now they entered a pine-forest, dark, damp,
and cold.   Once more the guide paused, and sent
a falcon-glance upwards to where the girl stood,
and the little village spread itself out smilingly on
the narrow mountain plateau in the full glow of
the morning sun, which as yet could hardly steal a
sidelong ray into the close, grave-like twilight of
the gorge.   "Thou needn't look so defiant, there's
a way up as well as down," he muttered, and disappeared with the stranger.   As though in scorn of
the threat, the girl sent up a halloo, so shrilly repeated from every side, that a flying echo reached
even the silent depth of the fir-wood with a ghostly
ring, like the challenging cry of the chamois-hunter's
enemy, the fairy of the Oetz valley.

"Ay, thou may'st scream; I'll soon give it back
to thee," he threatened again; and throwing himself stiffly back, and supporting his neck with both
hands, he pealed forth, clear and shrill as a post-

THE VULTURE-MAIDEN.

A TALE OF THE TYROLESE ALPS.

FAR down in the depths of the Oetz valley, a traveller was passing. On the eagle heights of the giddy precipice above him, stood a maiden's form, no bigger than an Alpine rose when seen from below, yet sharply defined against the clear blue sky, the gleaming ice-peaks of the Ferner. There she stood firm and tranquil, though the mountain gusts tore and snatched at her, and looked without dizziness down into the depths where the Ache rushed roaring through the ravine, and a sunbeam slanting across its fine spray-mist painted glimmering rainbows on the rocky wall. To her, also, the traveller and his guide appeared minutely small as they crossed the narrow bridge, which thrown high over the Ache, looked from above like a mere straw. She could not hear what the two were saying, for out of those depths no sound could reach her but the thundering roar of the waters. She could not see that the guide, a trimly-attired cha-

horn, a cry of mocking and defiance up the moun-tain-side.

"She hears that, maybe?"

"Why do you call the girl up there the Vulture-maiden?" asked the stranger down in the moist, dim, rustling forest.

"Because, Sir, when she was only a child she took a vulture's nest, and fought the old bird," said the Tyrolese. "She is the strongest and handsomest girl in all the Tyrol, and terribly rich, and the lads let her drive them off, so that it's a shame to see. There's not one of them sharp enough to master her. She is as shy as a wild cat, and so strong that the boys declare no one can conquer her: if one of them comes too near, she knocks him down. Well, if ever I went up there after her, I'd conquer her, or I'd tear the chamois-tuft and feather from my hat with my own hands."

"Why have you not already tried your luck with her, if she is so rich and so handsome?" asked the traveller.

"Well, you see, I don't care for girls like that —girls that are half boys. It's true, she can't help herself. The old man—Stromminger is his name —is a regular wicked old fellow. In his time he was the best wrestler and fighter in the mountains, and it sticks to him still. He has often beaten the

girl cruelly and brought her up like a boy. She
has no mother, and never had one, for she was such
a big strong child that her mother could scarcely
bring her into the world, and died of it. That's
how it is the girl has grown up so wild and master-
ful."—This was what the Tyrolese down in the
ravine related to the stranger, and he had not deceived himself. The maiden who stood out yonder
above the precipice was Wallburga Stromminger,
daughter of the powerful "chief-peasant," also
called the Vulture-maiden; and he had spoken truly,
she deserved this name. Her courage and strength
were boundless as though eagle's wings had borne
her, her spirit rugged and inaccessible as the jagged
peaks where the eagles build their nests, and where
the clouds of heaven are rent asunder.

Wherever anything dangerous was to be done,
there from her childhood upwards, was Wally to be
found, putting the lads to shame. As a child even
she was wild and impetuous as her father's young
bull, which she had known how to subdue. When
she was scarcely fourteen years old, a peasant had
descried on a rugged precipice a golden vulture's
nest with one young one, but no one in the village
dared venture to seize it. Then the head-peasant,
scoffing at the valiant youth of the place, declared
he would make his Wallburga do it. And sure

enough Wally was ready for the deed, to the horror of the women and the vexation of the lads. "It is a tempting of Providence," said the men. But Stromminger must have his jest; all the world must learn by experience that the race of Stromminger down to the children's children might seek its match in vain.

"You shall see that a Stromminger girl is worth ten of you lads," he said laughing to the peasants, who streamed together to witness the incredible feat. Many grieved for the beautiful and stately young life that might perhaps fall a sacrifice to the father's boasting; still, everyone wished to see. As the precipice to which the nest clung was almost perpendicular, and no human foot could tread it, a rope was fastened round Wally's waist. Four men, foremost amongst whom was her father, held it, but it was horrible to the lookers-on to see the courageous child, armed only with a knife, walk boldly to the edge of the plateau, and with a vigorous spring let herself down into the abyss. If the knot of the rope should give way, if the vulture should tear her in pieces, if in her descent she should dash out her brains against some unnoticed crag? It was a God-forsaken act of Stromminger's so to risk the life of his own child. Meanwhile Wally sailed fearlessly through the air, till midway

down the precipice she exultingly greeted the young
vulture, who ruffled his downy feathers, and piping,
gnawed with his shapeless beak at his strange
visitor. Hardly pausing to consider, she seized the
bird which now raised a lamentable cry with her
left hand and tucked it under her arm. There was
a rushing sound in the air, and in the same instant
a dark shadow came over her, a roaring filled her
ears, and a storm of blows fell like hail upon her
head. Her one thought was "The eyes—save the
eyes," and pressing her face closely against the
rock, she hit blindly with the knife in her right
hand at the raging bird that threw itself upon her
with its sharp beak, its claws and wings. Meanwhile the men above hastily drew in the rope. Still
for a time during the ascent, the battle in the air
continued; then suddenly the vulture gave way,
and plunged into the abyss—Wally's knife must
have wounded it. Wally however came up bleeding, her face torn by the rocks, and holding in her
arms the young bird, that at no price would she
have relinquished.

"But, Wally," cried the assembled people, "why
didn't thou let the young one go, then the vulture
would have loosed its hold." "Oh," she said simply,
"the poor thing can't fly yet, and if I had let him go,
he'd have fallen down the precipice and been killed."

This was the first and only time in her whole life that her father gave her a kiss; not because he was touched by Wally's noble compassion for the helpless creature, but because she had performed an heroic action that would reflect honour on the illustrious race of Stromminger.

Such was the maiden who stood out now on the projecting rock, where the foot could hardly find room to rest, and dreamily looked down into the ravine over which she hung; for often, with all her impetuosity, a strange stillness would come over her, and she would gaze sadly before her, as though she saw something for which she longed, and which she yet might not attain. It was an image that always remained the same, whether she saw it in the grey morning twilight, or in the golden glow of noon, in the evening red, or in the pale moonlight, and for a year it had followed her wherever she went or stood, below in the valley, or above on the mountain. And when, as now, she was out and alone, and her large chamois-eyes, at once wild and shy, wandered across to the white-gleaming glaciers, or down into the shadow-filled gorge where the Ache thundered on its way, still she sought him whom the image resembled; and when now and then a traveller, minutely small in the distance, glided past below, she thought, "That may be he,"

and a strange joy came to her in the fancy that she
had seen him, even though she could distinguish
nothing but a human form, no bigger than a moving image in a peep-show. And now as those two
wayfarers passed along, of whom the one enquired
about her, and the other threatened her, she thought
again, "It may be he." Her bosom seemed too
tight for her beating heart, her lips parted, and like
a lark set free, her joy soared up in a pealing song.
And as the hunter in the wood below heard its
dying echo, so an echo of his reply reached her,
and she listened with an intoxicated ear—it might
be *his* voice! and a blushing reflection of her warm
rush of feeling spread itself over the wild, defiant
face. She could not hear that the song was a song
of scorn and defiance. Had she known it, she would
have clenched her sinewy fist, she would have tried
the strength of her arm, and over her face dark
shadows would have passed, till it grew pale as the
glaciers after sunset. But now she sat down on the
stone that supported her, and swinging her feet as they
hung over the abyss, she rested her graceful head
on her hands, and gave herself up to dreaming over
again all the strange things that had happened that
first time that she ever saw him.

CHAPTER I.

Joseph, the Bear-hunter.

IT was at Whitsuntide, just a year before, that her father had taken her to Sölden for the confirmation; thither the bishop came every other year, because there is a high-road that leads to Sölden. She felt a little ashamed, for she was already sixteen years old, and so tall. Her father would not let her be confirmed before; he thought that with it would come at once love-makings and suitors—and time enough for that! Now she was afraid that the others would laugh at her. But no one took any notice: the whole village when they arrived was in excitement, for it was said that Joseph Hagenbach of Sölden had slain the bear that had shown itself up in Vintschgau, and for which the young men in all the country round had watched in vain. Then Joseph had set out across the mountains, and by Friday last he had already got him. The messenger from Schnalser had brought the news early, and Joseph himself was soon to follow. The peasants of Sölden, who were waiting in front of the Church, were full of pride that it should be a Söldener that had performed the dangerous deed, and talked of nothing but Joseph, who was indisputably the finest and strongest lad in all the mountains, and a shot without a rival. The girls listened admiringly to the tales of Joseph's heroic deeds, how no mountain was too steep for him, no road too long, no gulf too wide, and no danger too great; and when a pale, sickly-looking woman came towards them across the village-green, they all rushed up to her and wished her joy of the son who had won such glory.

"He's a good one, thy Joseph," said the men cordially; "he's one from whom all may take example." "If only thy husband had lived to see this day, how rejoiced he would have been," said the women.

"No, no one would ever believe," cried one quaintly, "that such a fine fellow was thy son—not looking at thee."

The woman smiled, well-pleased. "Yes, he's a fine-grown lad, and a good son, there can't be a better. And yet, if you'll believe it, I never have an hour's peace for him; there's not a day that I don't expect to see him brought home with his limbs all broken. It's a cross to bear!"

The religious procession now appeared upon the place, and put an end to the talk. The people thronged into the little church with the white-robed, gaily-wreathed children, and the sacred office began.

But the whole time Wally could think of nothing but Joseph, the bear-slayer, and of all the wonderful things he must have done, and of how splendid it was to be so strong and so courageous, and to be held in such great respect by every one, so that no one could get the better of him. If only he would come now, whilst she was in Sölden, so that she also might see him; she was really quite burning to see him.

At length the confirmation was over, and the children received the final blessing. Suddenly, on the green outside in front of the church, there was a sound of wild shouting and hurrahs. "He has him, he has the bear!" Scarcely had the bishop spoken the last words of the blessing when every one rushed out, and joyfully surrounded a young chamois-hunter, who, accompanied by a troop of fine and handsome lads from the Schnalser valley and from Vintschgau, was striding across the green. But handsome as his comrades might be, there was not one of them that came near him. He towered above them all, and was so beautiful—as beautiful as a picture. It seemed almost as though he shone with light from afar; he looked like the St. George in the church. Across his shoulders he carried the bear's fell, whose grim paws dangled over his broad chest. He walked as grandly as the emperor, and never took but one step when the others took two, and yet he was always ahead of them; and they made as much ado about him as though he had been the emperor indeed, dressed in a chamois-hunter's clothes. One carried his gun, another his jacket; all was wild excitement, shouting and huzza-ing—he alone remained composed and tranquil.

He went modestly up to the priest, who came towards him from the church, and took off his gar-landed hat. The bishop, who was a stranger, made the sign of the cross over him and said, "The Lord was mighty in thee, my son! With his help thou hast performed what none other could accomplish. Men must thank thee—but thou, thank thou the Lord!"

All the women wept with emotion, and even Wally had wet eyes. It was as though the spirit of devotion that had failed her in church, first came to her now, as she saw the stately hunter bow his proud head beneath the priest's benedictory hand. Then the bishop withdrew, and now Joseph's first enquiry was, "Where is my mother? Is she not here?"

"Yes, yes," she cried, "here am I," and fell into her son's arms.

Joseph clasped her tightly. "See, little mother," he said, "I should have been sorry for thy sake not to come back again. Thou dear little mother, thou'd never have known how to get on without me, and I too should have been loth to die without giving thee one more kiss."

Ah, it was beautiful, the way he said it! Wally had quite a strange feeling—a feeling as though she could envy the mother who rested so contentedly in the loving embrace of the son, and clung so tenderly to the powerful man. All eyes rested with delight on the pair, but an unutterable sensation filled Wally's heart.

"But tell us now, tell us how it all happened."

"Yes, yes, I'll tell you," he said laughing, and flung the bearskin on to the ground, so that all might see it. They made a circle round him, and the village landlord had a cask of his best ale brought out and tapped on the green; for one must drink after church, and above all on such an extra occasion as this, and the little inn-parlour could never have held such an unusual concourse of people. The men and women naturally pressed close round the speaker, and the newly-confirmed children climbed on to benches, and up into trees, that they might see over their heads. Wally was foremost of all in a fir-tree, where she could look straight down upon Joseph; but the others wanted her place; there was some noise and struggling because she would not give way, and "Saint George" looked up at them. His sparkling eyes fell upon Wally's face, and remained smilingly fixed on it for a moment. All Wally's blood rushed to her head, and she could hear her heart beating in her very ears with her intense fright. In all her life before she had never been so frightened, and she had not an idea why! She heard only the half of what Joseph was relating, there was such a singing in her ears; all the while she was thinking, "Suppose he were to look up again?" And she could not have told whether she wished it or dreaded it most. And yet, when in the course of his story it did once happen again, she turned away quickly and ashamed, as though she had been found out in something wrong. Was it wrong to have looked at him so? It might be, and yet she could not leave off, though she trembled so incessantly that she was afraid he might notice it. But he noticed nothing; what did he care for the child up there in the tree? He had looked up once or twice as he might have looked at a squirrel—nothing further. She said so to herself, and a strange sorrow stole over her. Never before had she felt as she did to-day; she was only thankful that she had drunk no wine on the road;

she might have thought that it had got into her head.

In her confusion she began playing with her rosary. It was a beautiful new one of red coral, with a chased cross of pure silver, that her father had given her for her confirmation. All of a sudden as she turned and twisted it, the string broke and, like drops of blood, the red beads rolled down from the tree. "That is a bad sign," an inner voice whispered to her, "old Luchard doesn't like it—that anything should break when one is thinking of something!" Of something! Of what then had she been thinking? She turned it over in her mind, but she could not discover. Precisely she had been thinking of nothing in particular. Why then should she be so troubled by the string breaking just at that moment? She felt as though the sun had suddenly paled, and a cold wind were blowing over her; but not a leaf was stirring, and the icebound horizon glittered in the radiant sunlight. The shadow of a cloud had passed—within her—or without her? How could she tell?

Joseph meanwhile had finished relating his adventure, and had shown round the purse containing the forty florins paid by the Tyrolese government as the reward for shooting a bear, and there was no end to the handshakings and congratulations.

Only Wally's father held sullenly aloof. It angered him that any one should accomplish a great and heroic deed; no one in the world had any right to be strong but himself and his daughter. During thirty years he had been esteemed, without dispute, the strongest man in the whole range of mountains, and he could not bear now to find himself growing old, and obliged to make way for a younger generation. When, however, someone said to Joseph that it was no wonder he should be such a strong fellow—he had it from his father who had been the best shot and the best wrestler in the whole place —then the old man could contain himself no longer, but broke in with a thundering "Oho! no need to bury a man before he's dead!"

Everyone fell back at the threatening voice. "It's Stromminger!" they said, half-frightened.

"Ay, it is Stromminger, who's alive still, and who never knew till this moment that Hagenbach had been the best wrestler in the place. With his tongue, if you like, but with nothing else!"

Joseph turned round like a wounded wild cat, glaring at Stromminger with flaming eyes. "Who says that my father was a boaster?"

"I say it, the head-peasant of the Sonnenplatte, and I know what I'm saying, for I've laid him flat a dozen times, like a sack."

"It is false," cried Joseph, "and no man shall blacken my father's name."

"Joseph, be quiet," the people whispered about him, "it's the head-peasant—thou mustn't make a quarrel with him."

"Head-peasant here, head-peasant there! If God in Heaven were to come down to blacken my father's name, I wouldn't put up with it. I know very well, my father and Stromminger had many a wrestling-bout together, because he was the only one who could stand up with Stromminger. And he threw Stromminger just as often as Stromminger threw him."

"It's not true!" shouted Stromminger, "thy father was a weak fool compared to me. If any of you old fellows have a spark of honour, you'll say so too—and thou, if thou doesn't believe it after that, I'll knock it into thee!" At the word "fool" Joseph had sprung like a madman, close up to Stromminger. "Take thy words back, or—"

"Heavens above us!" shrieked the women. "Let be, Joseph," said his mother soothingly, "he's an old man, thou mustn't lay hands on him."

"Oho!" cried Stromminger, purple with rage, "you'd make me out an old dotard, would you? Stromminger is none so old and weak yet but he can fight it out with a half-fledged stripling. Only come on, I'll soon show thee I've some marrow left in my bones. I'm not afraid of thee yet awhile, not if thou'd shot ten bears."

And like an enraged bull the strong old man threw himself on the young hunter, who in spite of himself gave way under the sudden and heavy spring. But he only staggered for a moment; his slender form was so firmly knit, was so supple in yielding, so elastic in rising again—like the lofty pines of his native soil, that grow with roots of iron in the naked rock, buffeted by all the winds of heaven and bearing up against their mountain-load of snow. As easily might Stromminger have up-rooted one of these trees, as have flung Joseph to the ground. And in fact, after a short struggle, Joseph's arms closely clasped Stromminger, tighten-ing round and almost choking him, till a deep groan came with his shortening breath, and he could not stir a hand. And now the young giant began to shake the old man, bending first on one side, then on the other, striving steadily, slowly but surely to force first one foot and then the other from under him, and so loosen his foothold by de-grees. The bystanders hardly dared to breathe as they watched the strange scene—almost as though they dared not look on at the felling of so old a tree. Now—now Stromminger has lost his footing—now he must fall—but no; Joseph held him up, bore him in his strong arms to the nearest bench and set him down on it. Then he quietly took out his handkerchief and dried the beads of sweat from Stromminger's brow.

"See, Stromminger," he said, "I've got the better of thee, and I might have thrown thee; but God forbid that I should bring an old man to shame. And now we will be good friends again; we bear no malice, Stromminger?"

He held out his hand, smiling goodhumouredly, but Stromminger struck it back with an angry scowl. "The devil pay thee out—thou scoundrel," he cried. "And you, all you Söldeners who have amused yourselves with seeing Stromminger made a laughing-stock for the children—you shall learn by experience who Stromminger is. I'll have nothing more to do with you, and grant no more time for payments—not if half Sölden were to starve for it."

He went up to the tree, where Wally still sat as in a nightmare, and pulled her by the gown. "Come down," he said, "thou'll get no dinner there. Not a Söldener shall ever see another kreuzer of mine." But Wally, who had rather fallen than got down from the tree, stood as if spell-bound with her eyes fixed almost beseechingly on Joseph. She thought he must see how it pained her to go away; she felt

2*

as though he must take her hand in his, and say, "Only stay with me: thou belong'st to me, and I to thee, and to no other!" But he stood still in the midst of a knot of men who were whispering together in dismay, for many in the village owed money to Stromminger, whose wealth circulated in the very veins of the whole neighbourhood.

"Well—wilt thou go on?" said Stromminger, giving the girl a push, and she had to obey him whether for weal or woe; but her lips trembled, her breast heaved painfully; she flung a glance of powerless anger at her father; he drove her before him like a calf. So they went on for a few steps; then they heard some one following them, and turning round, there stood Joseph with a couple of peasants behind him.

"Stromminger," he said, "don't be so headstrong. You can never go, you and the girl, all that long way to the Sonnenplatte, without eating anything."

He stood close to Wally; she felt his breath as he spoke, his eyes rested on her, his hand lay compassionately on her shoulder; she knew not how it happened—he was so good, so dear—and she felt as she did when, taking the vulture's nest, the rushing sound of its wings suddenly filled her ears, and sight and hearing went from her. Even so, something overwhelming to her young heart, lay in his presence, in his touch. She had not trembled when the mighty bird hovered above her, darkening the sun with his broad pinions, she had known how to defend herself calmly and bravely; but now she trembled from head to foot, and stood bewildered and confused.

"Get off!" cried Stromminger, and clenched his fist at Joseph, "I'll hit thee in the face if thou doesn't let me be—I will, if it cost me my life."

"Well—if you won't, you won't, and so let it be, —but you're a fool, Stromminger," said Joseph calmly, and he turned round and went back with the others.

Now no one tried to detain them; they walked on unmolested, farther—at each step farther away from Joseph. Wally looked round, and still for a time she could see his head towering above the others, she could still hear the confused sound of voices and of laughter on the green before the church. She could not yet believe that she was really gone, that she should not see Joseph again— perhaps never again. Now they turned a corner of the rock and all was hidden, the village green with all the people and Joseph—and every thing, every thing was gone. Then suddenly there came upon her, as it were, a revelation of a great joy of which she had had one glimpse, and which was lost to her for ever now. She looked around as though imploring help in her soul's need, in this new, this unknown anguish. And there was none to answer her and to say, "Be patient, presently all will be well!" Dead and motionless were the rocks and cliffs all around, dead and motionless the Ferner looked down upon her. What did they care, they who had seen worlds come and worlds pass away, for this poor little trembling woman's heart? Her father walked on at her side, silent as though he were a moving rock. And he it was that was guilty of all. He was a wicked, hard, cruel man; there was not a creature in the world that took any interest in her. And while she thought all this, struggling with herself, she walked on mechanically farther and farther in advance of her father, up hill and down hill, as though she wished to walk off her heart's pain. The scorching sun glared on the blank wall of rock, she strove for breath, her tongue clove to the roof of her mouth, all her veins throbbed; suddenly her strength gave way, she threw herself on the ground and broke into loud sobs.

"Oho! what's all this about?" exclaimed Stromminger in the greatest astonishment, for never since her earliest infancy had he seen his daughter weep. "Art out of thy wits?"

Wally made no reply; she gave herself up to the wild outbreak of her soul's suffering.

"Speak, will thee? open thy mouth or—"

Then from her throbbing, raging heart, like a mountain torrent from the cleft rock, she poured forth the whole truth, overwhelming the old man with the rush and ferment of her passion. She told him everything, for truthful she had always been and unaccustomed to lying. She told him that Joseph had pleased her, that she felt such a love for him as no one in the world had ever felt before, that she had been rejoicing so in the thought of talking to him, and that if Joseph had only heard how strong she was and how she had already done all sorts of strong things, he would certainly have danced with her and he would certainly have fallen in love with her too; and now her father had deprived her of it all, because he must needs fall upon Joseph like a madman; and now she was a laughing-stock and a disgrace, so that Joseph to the last day of his life would never look at her again. But that was always the way with her father, he was always hard and mad with everyone, so that everywhere he was called the wicked Stromminger—and now she must atone for it all.

Then suddenly Stromminger spoke. "I've had enough of this," he cried. There was a whistling through the air, and such a blow from her father's stick crashed down upon Wally that she thought her spine was broken; she turned pale and bowed her head. It was as hail falling on the scarce opened blossom of her soul. For a moment she was in such pain that she could not stir; bitter tears forced themselves through her closed eyes, like sap from a broken stem; otherwise she lay still as death. Stromminger waited by her muttering curses, as a drover stands by a heifer that, felled by a blow, can do no more.

Around them all was still and lonely, no voice of bird, no rustling of trees broke the silence. On the narrow rocky path where father and daughter stood, no tree ever bore a leaf, no bird ever built its nest. A thousand years ago the elements must have warred here in fearful conflict, and far as the eye could reach nothing could be seen but the giant wrecks of the wild tumult. But now the fires were burnt out that had rent the ground, and the waters subsided that had swept away the strong ones of the earth in their raging flood. There they lay hurled one upon another, the motionless giants; the mighty powers that had moved them lay slumbering now, and peace as of the grave lay over all as over monuments of the dead, and pure and still as heavenward aspirations the white glaciers rose high above them. Only man, ever-restless man, carried on even here his never ending strife, and with his suffering destroyed the sublime peace of nature.

At last Wally opened her eyes and gathered her strength to go on; no further lamentation passed her lips, she looked at her father strangely, as though she had never seen him before; her tears were dried up.

"Thou may guess now what'll come of it, if thou thinks any more of yon scoundrel that made thy father a jest for children," said he, holding her by the arm, "for thou may know this, that I'd sooner fling thee down from the Sonnenplatte than let Joseph have thee."

"It is well," said Wally, with an expression that startled even Stromminger; such unflinching defiance lay in the simple words, in the tone in which they were spoken, in the glance of irreconcilable enmity which she threw at her father.

"Thou's a wicked—wicked thing," muttered he between his teeth.

"I have not stolen anything," she answered in the same tone.

"Only wait awhile—I'll pay thee out," he snarled.

"Yes, yes," she answered, nodding her head, as if to say, "only try it!" Then they said no more to each other the whole way back.

When they had reached home, and Wally had gone into her room to take off her holiday finery, old Luckard who had lived with her mother and her grandmother, and who had brought Wally up from her cradle, put her head in at the door. "Wally, hast been weeping?" she whispered.

"Why?" asked the girl with unwonted sharpness.

"There were tears on the cards—I laid out the pack of cards for thy confirmation; thou fell between two knaves and I was frightened at it; it was all as near as if it had happened to-day and close by."

"Like enough," said the girl indifferently, and laid away her mother's beautiful gown in the big wooden chest.

"Does anything ail thee, child?" asked the old woman. "Thou looks so ill and thou'st come home so early. Didn't thou dance?"

"Dance!" The girl laughed, a hard shrill laugh, as though one should strike a lute with a hammer till the strings ring back all jarred and jangled out of tune. "What have I to do with dancing."

"Something's happened to thee, child—tell me —perhaps I can help thee."

"None can help me," said Wally, and shut down

the lid of the chest as if she would bury in it all that was oppressing her. It was as though she were closing down the coffin-lid over all her youthful hopes.

"Go now," she said imperiously, as she had never spoken before, "I shall rest awhile."

"Jesus, Maria!" shrieked Luckard, "there lies thy rosary all broken. Where are the beads?"

"Lost."

"Oh! Lord! Lord! what ill luck! only the cross is left and the empty string. To break thy rosary on thy confirmation day! and tears on the cards besides! Our Father in Heaven! what will come of it?"

Thus lamenting, half pushed out by Wally, the old woman left the room, and Wally bolted the door after her. She threw herself on the bed and lay motionless, staring at the picture of the Holy Mother and at the crucifix which hung on the wall opposite. Should she pour out her sorrows to these? No! The Mother of God could bear her no good-will, otherwise she would not have let just her confirmation day above all others be so spoilt for her. Besides, she could not know what love-sorrows were, for she had known suffering only through her Son, and that was something quite different from what Wally felt. And the Lord Jesus Christ!

—He certainly did not trouble himself about love-stories; no one might dare to approach Him with such matters as these. All that He desired was that one should be always striving after the kingdom of Heaven. Ah! And all her young, wildly-beating heart was longing and yearning with every throb for the beloved, the best-beloved one down here on earth; the kingdom of Heaven was so far away and so strange, how could she strive after it in this moment when, for the first time, all powerful nature was imperiously claiming in her its right? With bitter defiance she gazed at the images of the Mother and Son, whose pity was for quite other griefs than hers, who demanded of her only what was impossible. She vouchsafed to them no further word, she was angry with them as a child is angry with its parents when they unjustly deny it some pleasure. Long she lay thus, her eyes fixed reproachfully on the holy images; but soon she saw before her only the dear and beautiful face of Joseph, and involuntarily she grasped her shoulder with her hand where his hand had lain, as though to keep firm hold of his momentary touch. And then she saw his mother again of whom she had been so jealous, and she lay once more in Joseph's arms, and he caressed her so fondly; and then Wally pushed the mother away and lay herself instead on Joseph's heart; and he held her clasped there, and she looked down into the depths of his black flaming eyes, and she tried to imagine what he would say, but she could think of nothing but, "Thou dear little one," as he had said, "Thou dear little mother." And what could be sweeter or dearer than that? Ah! what could the kingdom of Heaven, in which those Two up yonder wanted to have her, what could it be in comparison with the blessedness that she felt in only thinking of Joseph—and how much greater must the reality be!

There was a tap at her window, and she started up as if from a dream. It was the young vulture which she had taken two years before from the nest, and which was as faithfully attached to her as a dog. She could leave him quite free, he never hurt anyone, and flew after her with his clipped wings as best he could. She opened the little window, he slipped in and looked trustingly at her with his yellow eyes. She scratched his neck gently and played with his strong wings, now spreading them out, now folding them together again. A cool air blew in through the open window. The sun had already sunk low behind the mountains, the narrow casement framed the peaceful picture of the mountain tops veiled in blue mist. In herself too all grew more peaceful; the evening air revived her spirit. She took the bird on her shoulder. "Come, Hans," she said, "we are doing nothing, as though there were no work in the world." The faithful bird had brought her wonderful comfort. She had taken it for her own from the steep cliff where no one else would venture; she had fought its mother for life or death, she had tamed it and it belonged wholly to her. "And *he* will also one day be mine," said an inward voice, as she clasped the bird to her bosom.

CHAPTER II.

Unbending.

THIS was the short story of love and sorrow, whose pain even now awoke again in the young heart as she looked down into the valley, thinking to see Joseph who so often passed along it, and never found the way up to her. She wiped her forehead, for the sun was beginning to burn, and she had already mowed the whole meadow-land from the house up to the "Sonnenplatte;" so the point on which she stood was called, because rising high above all around, it ever caught the earliest rays of the morning sun. From it the village took its name.

"Wally, Wally," some one now called from behind her, "come to thy father, he's something to say to thee," and old Luckard came towards her from the house. Her father had sent for her? What could he want? Never since their adventure in Sölden had he spoken with her excepting of what concerned the day's work. Wavering between fear and reluctance she rose and followed the old woman.

"What does he want?" she asked.

"Great news," said Luckard, "look there!"

Wally looked, and saw her father standing before the house, and with him a young peasant of the place named Vincenz, with a big nosegay in his button hole. He was a dark, robust fellow whom Wally had known from her childhood as a reserved and stubborn man. He had never bestowed a kindly word on anyone but Wally, to whom from her school-days upwards he had shown a special goodwill. A few months previously both his parents had died within a short time of each other; now he was independent, and next to Stromminger the richest peasant in the country side. The blood stood still in Wally's veins, for she already knew what was coming.

"Vincenz wants to marry thee," said her father; "I've said 'yes,' and next month we'll have the wedding." Having thus spoken he turned on his heel and went into the house as if there were nothing more to be said.

Wally stood silent for a moment as though thunderstruck; she must collect herself, she must consider what was to be done. Vincenz meanwhile confidently stepped up to her with the intention of putting his arm round her waist. But she sprang back with a cry of terror, and now she knew well enough what it was she had to do.

"Vincenz," she said, trembling with misery, "I beg of thee to go home. I can never be thy wife—never. Thou wouldn't have my father force me to it. I tell thee once for all I cannot love thee."

A look brief as lightning flashed across Vincenz's face; he bit his lips, and his black eyes were fixed with passionate eagerness on Wally. "So thou doesn't love me? But I love thee, and I'll lay my life on it that I'll have thee too. I've got thy father's consent and I'll never give it back, and I've a notion thou'll come to change thy mind yet if thy father wills it."

"Vincenz," said Wally, "if thou'd been wise thou'd not have spoken like that, for thou'd have known I'll never have thee now. What I will not do, none can force me to do—that thou may know once for all. And now go home, Vincenz; we've nothing more to say to each other," and she turned short away from him and went into the house.

"Oh, thou!" Vincenz called out after her in angry pain, clenching his fist. Then he checked himself. "Well," he murmured between his teeth, "I can wait—and I *will* wait."

Wally went straight to her father. He was sitting all bent together over his accounts and turned round slowly as she entered. "What is it?" he said.

The sun shone through the low window and

threw its full beams on Wally, so that she stood as though wrapped in glory before her father. Even he was amazed at the beauty of his child as she stood before him at that moment.

"Father," she began quietly, "I only wanted to tell you that I will not marry Vincenz."

"Indeed!" cried Stromminger, starting up. "Is that it? Thou won't marry him?"

"No, father, I don't like him."

"Indeed! and did I ask thee if thou liked him?"

"No, I tell it you plainly, unasked."

"And I tell thee too unasked that in four weeks thou'll marry Vincenz whether thou likes him or not. I've given him my word, and Stromminger never takes his word back. Now get thee gone."

"No, father," said the girl, "things can't be settled in that way. I'm no head of cattle to let myself be sold or promised as the master pleases. It seems to me I also have a word to say when it has to do with my marriage."

"No, that thou hasn't, for a child belongs to her father as much as a calf or a heifer, and must do what its father orders."

"Who says that, father?"

"Who says so? It's said in the Bible," and an ominous flush rose on Stromminger's face.

"It says in the Bible that we are to honour and

love our parents, but not that we are to marry a man when it goes against us merely because our father orders it. See, father, if it could do you any good for me to marry Vincenz, if it could save you from death or from misery—I'd do it willingly, and even if I were to break my heart over it. But you're a rich man that need ask nothing of anyone; it must be all one to you whom I marry; and you give me to Vincenz out of pure spite, that I may not marry Joseph, whom I love, and who would certainly have loved me if he could have got to know me; and it's cruel of you, father, and it says nowhere in the Bible that a child should put up with that."

"Thou—thou pert thing, I'll send thee to the priest; he'll teach thee what the Bible says."

"It will be no good, father; and if you sent me to ten priests, and if they all ten told me that I must obey you in this, I yet wouldn't do it."

"And I tell thee thou *shall* do it so sure as my name is Stromminger. Thou shall do it, or I'll drive thee out of house and home and disinherit thee."

"That you can do, father, I'm strong enough to earn my own bread. Yes, father, give everything to Vincenz—only not me."

"Foolish nonsense," said Stromminger perplexed. "Shall people say of me that Stromminger cannot even master his own child? Thou shall marry Vincenz; if I have to thrash thee into church, thou shall."

"And even if you thrashed me into church I'd still say no, at the altar. You may strike me dead, but you cannot thrash that 'Yes' out of me; and even if you could, sooner would I fling myself down from the cliff, than I'd go home with a man I've no love for."

"Now listen," cried Stromminger; his broad forehead was cleft as it were, with a swelling blue vein that ran across it, his whole face was suffused, his eyes bloodshot. "Now listen, thou'd better not drive me mad. Thou's already had enough of my cudgel; now give in, or between us things will come to a bad end!"

"Things came to a bad end between us a year ago, father. For when you beat me so that time on my confirmation day, then I felt all was at an end between us. And see, father, since then it's been all one to me whether you are bad to me or good, whether you treat me well or strike me dead —it's all one to me. I have no heart left for you. You're no dearer to me than the Similaun-, or Vernagt-, or Murzoll-glacier."

A stifled cry of rage broke from Stromminger. Half-stupified he had listened to the girl's words, but now, incapable of speech, he sprang upon her, seized her by the waist, swung her from the ground high over his head, and shook her till his own breath failed; then flinging her to the ground he set his heavy heel studded with nails upon her breast. "Unsay what thou has said," he gasped, "or I'll crush thee like a worm."

"Do it," said the girl, her eyes fixed steadily on her father. She breathed hard, for her father's foot weighed on her like lead, but she did not stir; not so much as an eyelash trembled.

Stromminger's power was broken. He had threatened what he could not perform, for at the thought of crushing the fair and innocent breast of his child his anger faded, he grew suddenly calm. He was conquered. Almost staggering he drew back his foot.

"Nay, I'll not end my days in a prison," he said gloomily, and sank exhausted into his chair.

Wally got up, she was pale as death, her eyes were tearless, lustreless, like a stone. She waited passively for what might come next. Stromminger sat for a minute in bitter reflection, then he spoke in hoarse tones.

"I cannot kill thee, but since Similaun and Murzoll are dear to thee as thy father, by Similaun and Murzoll thou may remain for the future, thou may belong to them. Thou shall never more stretch thy feet under my board. Thou shall go and mind the cattle up on the Hochjoch, till thou's found out it's better to be in Vincenz's warm home, than in the snow drift of the glacier. Tie up thy bundle, for I'll see no more of thee. Go up early to-morrow. I'll let the Schnalser people know, and send the cattle after thee next week by the boy. Take bread and cheese enough to last till the beasts come; Klettenmaier will guide thee up there. Now take thyself off. These are my last words and by *these* I'll stand."

"It is well, father," said Wally softly; she bowed her head, and quitted her father's room.

CHAPTER III.

Outcast.

"Up on the Hochjoch!" It was a fearful sentence. For in the inhospitable regions of the Hochjoch there is none of the joyous life of the lower pastures, where the sweet aromatic air resounds with the tinkle of bells, with the calls of the herdsmen and mountain girls—here are eternal winter, and the stillness of death. Sadly and gently as a mother kisses the pale forehead of her dead child, so the sun kisses these cold glaciers. Scanty meadows, the last clinging vestiges of organic life penetrate, as though lost, the wintry desert, till the last shoot perishes, the last drop of rising sap is frozen; it is the slow extinction of nature. But the frugal peasant utilises even these niggard remains; he sends his flocks up to graze on what they may find there, and the straying sheep tempted to reach after a plant which has wandered hither from a milder region, not unfrequently falls into some crevice in the ice.

Here it was that the child of the proud chief peasant, whose possessions extended ·for miles in every direction and reached up even to the clouds, must spend her bloom in everlasting winter. While on the lower earth May-breezes were blowing, the rising sap opening every bud, the birds building their nests, and all things stirring in joyous unison, she must take the herdsman's staff and quit the spring-meadows for the desert of the glaciers above; and only when autumn winds should be sighing and winter preparing to descend into the valley, might she also return thither, as though she had been sold to winter, life and limb.

No one of the peasants of the neighbourhood would send his shepherds up there, but they let out the meadows to the Schnalser people who lay nearer to the ridge on the farther side, and they sent a few half-wild, weather-beaten fellows, who clothed themselves in skins and lived miles asunder in stone cabins like hermits; and now Stromminger, who hitherto had always leased his pastures, condemned his own child to lead the life of a Schnalser herdsman. But from Wally's lips came no complaint; she prepared herself in silence for her mountain journey. Early in the morning, long before sunrise, whilst her father, the men, and the maids were still sleeping, Wally set out from her father's house for the mountain. Only old Luckard, "who had known it all beforehand from the cards" and who had passed the night with Wally helping her make up her bundle, stuck a sprig of rue in her hat as a farewell-token, and went part of the way with her. The old woman wept as if escorting the dead to the grave. Klettenmaier came behind with the pack. He was a faithful old servant, the only one that had grown grey in Stromminger's service, because he was deaf and did not hear when his master stormed and swore. This was the guide her father had selected for Wally. Luckard went with her till the road began a steep ascent. Then she took leave of them and turned back, for she had to be home in time to prepare the first meal.

Wally climbed the hill and looked down upon the road along which the old woman went crying in her apron, and even her heart almost failed her. Luckard had always been good to her; though she was old and feeble, at least she had loved Wally. Presently the old woman turned once more and pointed above her head. Wally's eyes followed the direction of her finger, and behold! something floated towards the mountain heights clumsily, uncertainly through the air, like a paper kite when the wind fails, now flying on a little way, then falling, and with difficulty rising again. The vulture with his clipped wings had painfully fluttered the whole way after her; but now his strength seemed to give way and he could only scramble along, flapping his pinions.

"Hansl!—oh, my Hansl!—how could I forget thee!" cried Wally, springing like a chamois from rock to rock the shortest way back to fetch the faithful bird. Luckard stood still till Wally once more reached the narrow path, then greeted her again as if after a long separation. At last Hansl too was reached, and Wally took him in her arms and pressed him to her heart like a child. Since last evening the bird was so identified in all her thoughts with Joseph, that it seemed almost as if it were a dumb medium between him and her; or as though Joseph had changed into the vulture, and in holding Hansl she clasped him in her arms.

As an ardent faith creates its own visible symbols to bring near to itself the unattainable and the remote and to seize the intangible, and as to faith a wooden cross and a painted image become miraculous—so ardent love creates its own symbols, to which it clings when the beloved one is far off, unattainable. Even so Wally derived now a wonderful consolation from her bird. "Come, Hansl," she said tenderly, "thou shall go with me up to the Ferner; we two will never be parted more."

"But, child," said old Luckard, "thou never can take the vulture up there, he'd die of hunger.

Thou's no meat for him up there, and creatures like him eat nothing else."

"That is true," said Wally sadly, "but I can't part from the bird; I must have something with me up there in the wilderness. And I can't leave him alone at home either; who'd look after him and take care of him when I'm away?"

"Oh! for that thou may be easy," cried Luckard, "I'll look after him well enough."

"Ay, but he'll not follow thee," said Wally; "thou'rt not used to his ways."

"Nay, let me have him," said Luckard. "All this long time I've taken care of thee, surely I can take care of the bird. Give him me here, I'll carry him home," and she pulled the vulture out of Wally's arms. But it would not do; the noble bird set himself on the defensive, and pecked so angrily at Luckard that she was frightened, and let go. It was of no use for her to think of taking him home with her.

"Thou sees," cried Wally joyfully, "he'll not leave me; I must keep him, come what will. I was once called the Vulture-maiden and the Vulture-maiden I must still remain. O, my Hansl, as long as we two are together, we shall want for nothing. I'll tell thee what, Luckard, I'll let his wings grow

now, he'll not fly away from me, and then he can
find food for himself up yonder."

"God bless thee, then, take him with thee. I'll
send thee up some fresh and salt meat by the boy,
thou can give him that till he can fly abroad." And
so it was settled. Wally took the vulture under
her arm like a hen, and parted from Luckard who
began to cry afresh. But Wally, without further
delay, went up the mountain again after the guide,
who had meanwhile gone on ahead.

In two hours they reached Vent, the last village
before entering the realms of ice. Wally mounted
the hill above Vent; here began the path to the
Hochjoch. Once more she paused, and leaning on
her Alpenstock looked down on the quiet, still half-
dreaming village, and over the lake beyond, and the
last houses of the Oetz valley, to the farms of
Rofen which, lying almost at the foot of the ever-
advancing, ever-receding Hochvernagtferners, seemed
defiantly to say to it, "Crush us!"—even as Wally
yesterday had defied her father. And like her
father the Hochvernagt each time withdrew its
mighty foot, as though it could not bear to destroy
the home of its brave mountain children, "the Klötze
of Rofen."

While she thus stood, looking down on the utmost dwellings of man before mounting to the

desert beyond the clouds, there rose from the church-tower of Vent the sound of the bell for matins. Out of the door of the little parsonage, where the buds of the mountain-pink tapped the window in the morning breeze, came the priest and went with folded hands to his pious duty in the church. Here and there the wooden houses opened their sleepy eyes, and one figure after another coming out, stretched itself and took its way slowly to the church. Carefully and losing no tone by the way, the wind-winged angels bore the pious sound up the slope, and it rang in Wally's ear like the voice of a child that prays. And as a child arouses its mother by its sweet lisping, so the peal from Vent seemed to have aroused the sun. He opened his mighty eye, and the rays of his first glance shot over the mountains, an immeasurable shaft of flame that crowned the eastern heights. The dim grey of the twilight sky suddenly lighted up to a transparent blue, each moment the beam grew broader in the heavens, and at length mounted in full splendour over the cloud-veiled peaks, and turned his flaming countenance lovingly to earth. The mountains threw off their misty shrouds, and bathed their naked forms in streams of light. Deep down in the ravines the clouds heaved and rolled, as though they had sunk down thither from the pure heaven

above. In the air was a rushing as of wild hymns
of joy, and the earth wept tears of blissful waking,
like a bride on her wedding morning; and like the
tears on the eyelashes of the bride, the dewdrops
quivered joyfully on each blade and spray. Joy
lay everywhere,—above on the mountain tops where
the dazzling rays were mirrored in the farseeing
eyes of the chamois,—below in the valley where the
lark soared, warbling, from amongst the springing corn.

Wally gazed intoxicated on the awakening world,
with eyes that could hardly take in the whole shining picture in its pure morning beauty. The vulture on her shoulder lifted its wings as though
longingly to greet the sun. Below in Vent, meanwhile, all was awakening to new life. From where
Wally stood she could see everything distinctly in
the clear morning light. The lads kissed the maidens
by the well. White smoke curled upwards from the
houses, vanishing without a trace in the serene
spring air, as a sorrowful thought loses itself in a
happy soul. On the green in front of the church
the men assembled in white Sunday shirt-sleeves,
their silver-mounted pipes in their mouths. It was
Whit-Monday, when all make holiday and rejoice.
Oh! holy Whitsuntide! just such a day must it have
been when the Spirit of the Lord fell on the dis-

ciples and enlightened them with divine illumination, that they might go forth into all the world and preach the Gospel of Love, preach it to open hearts, touched by the happy spring—for, in the spring-tide of the year appeared also the spring-tide of man—the religion of love. For her only who stood up there on the mountain was there no Whitsuntide, no revelation of love. In her no persuasive voice had quickened the gospel into life. A meaningless letter it had remained to her, a buried seed which needed the vivifying ray to make it spring up in her heart. No dew of peace fell on her from the deep blue heavens; the bird of prey on her shoulder was to her the only messenger of love.

At last Wally broke away from her dreamy contemplation. She gave one farewell glance to the merry, noisy villagers, then she turned to climb the silent snow fields of the Hochjoch—in banishment.

CHAPTER IV.

Murzoll's Child.

FOR five hours did Wally continue to ascend; now over whole fields of fragrant Alpine plants, now sinking ankle-deep in snow-fields, or crossing broad moraines. Last night's sleeplessness lay heavily upon her limbs, and she almost despaired of ever reaching the end of her journey. Her hands and feet trembled, for to struggle for life during five hours against so steep an ascent is hard work. Large drops stood on Wally's brow, when suddenly as by a magic stroke she stood before a dense wall of cloud. She had turned an angle of the rock which hid the sun, and now thick mists enveloped her and an icy breath dried the sweat from her forehead. Her foot slipped at every step, for the ground was like glass; she stood upon ice, she had stepped upon the Murzoll glacier, the highest ridge of the serrated Hochjoch. Nothing grew here but starveling mountain-grass between clefts in the snow; around were the blue gleaming ice-crevasses, the virgin snow-flats, untrodden this year by foot of man or beast. Mid-winter! Wally shuddered at its icy touch. This was the forecourt to Murzoll's ice-palace, of which so many tales are told in the Oetz valley, where the "phantom maidens" dwell, of whom old Luckard had related many a story to the little Wally in the long winter evenings when the snow-storms howled round the house. The air that blew on her now from those desolate walls of ice, those caves and dungeons, came to her with a ghostly thrill like a shudder out of her childhood, as though in very truth there dwelt the dark spirit of the glacier, with whom Luckard had so often frightened her to bed when she had been naughty.

Silently she walked on. At last her deaf guide halted by a low cabin built of stone, with a wide overhanging roof, a strong door of rough wood, and little slits instead of windows. Within were a couple of blackened stones for a hearth, and a bed of old rotten straw. This was the hut of the Schnalser herdsman, who had formerly found shelter here, and here Wally was now to dwell. She did not change countenance however at the sight of the comfortless hut; it was neither more nor less than a bad mountain cabin, there were many such, and she was used to hard living. It was not such things as these that could quench her resolute spirit; but she was exhausted to faintness; since yesterday she had gone through more than even

her unusual strength could bear. Mechanically she
helped the deaf man, whom Luckard had loaded
with a number of good things for Wally, to ar-
range a better bed, and to make the desolate hut
somewhat more habitable. Mechanically she eat
with him some of the food Luckard had sent. The
man saw that she was pale, and said compassionately,
"There, now thou's eaten something, lie down a
while and sleep. Thou needs it. I'll fetch thee up
some wood meanwhile to last thee a few days, then
I must go back, or I shall never be home by daylight, and thy father strictly ordered me to get back
to-day." He shook up a good bed of straw that
he had brought with him; she sank down on it
with half closed eyes and held out her hand grate-
fully.

"I'll not wake thee," he said. "In case thou'rt
still asleep when I go, I'll say goodbye to thee now.
Take care of thyself and don't be frightened. I'm
sorry for thee all alone up here; but, why didn't
thou obey thy father?"   •

Wally heard the last words as in a dream. The
deaf man left the cabin, shaking his head compassionately; the girl was already sound asleep.

Her breast heaved painfully, for even in her
sleep her past sorrow weighed on her like a mountain. And she dreamed of her father; he was

dragging her into church by her hair, and she thought that if only she had a knife so that she might cut off her hair she would be free. Then suddenly Joseph stood by her, and with one stroke he cut through the long plait, so that it remained in her father's hand; and while Joseph was struggling with her father she ran out and climbed to the height of the Sonnenplatte to throw herself into the torrent. But a terror came over her, and she hesitated; then again she heard her father close behind her,• and urged by despair she made the leap. She fell and fell, but could never reach the bottom, and suddenly she felt as if she were met from below by a gust of wind that supported and carried her upwards. So she floated, struggling always to keep the balance she continually feared to lose, up to the very summit of Murzoll. But she could gain no footing on the rock; a terrible whirlwind had seized her, and she strove in vain to cling to the bare precipice, like a ship that cannot reach the land. Black storm-clouds gathered together around her, through which Murzoll's snowy summit rose in ghostly whiteness. Fiery snakes shot through the black mass, the mountains quaked beneath a crashing thunder-clap, and flung whirling backwards and forwards between these mighty powers, a terror came over her that

4*

the tempest might cast her head downwards into the abyss. She bowed and turned, like a little ship on the swaying waves of the wind, striving only to keep her head uppermost. But suddenly her feet were raised and she felt that the weight of her head must carry her down, through the storm and thunder and the black darkness of the clouds; she would have cried for help, but could utter no sound— terror choked her voice. Then all at once she felt herself supported, she was on firm ground, she lay in a mountain cleft, as it seemed; but nó, it was no cleft, they were giant arms of stone that embraced her, and behold, out of the brightening clouds a mighty face of stone bent over her: it was the hoary countenance of Murzoll. His hair was of snow-covered fir trees, his eyes were ice, his beard was of moss and his eyebrows of edelweiss; on his brow was set as a diadem the crescent moon which shed its mild radiance over the white face; and the icy eyes shone with a ghostly light in its bluish rays. He gazed at the maiden with these cold eyes, piercing but unfathomable, and beneath their glance the drops of agony on her brow and the tears on her cheeks froze and fell down with a faint ringing sound like crystal beads. He pressed his stony lips to hers, and under the long kiss his mouth grew warm and dewy and blossomed with Alpine roses, and when Wally looked up at him again glacier streams flowed from the icy eyes down upon his mossy beard. The black clouds had cleared away and the breath of spring stirred the night.

Now Murzoll moved his lips, and his voice sounded like the dull roll of a distant avalanche. "Thy father has banished thee," he said, "I will receive thee as my child, for a heart of cold stone may more easily be moved than the hardened heart of man. Thou pleasest me, thou art one of mine; there is strength in thy nature as the rocks are strong. Wilt thou be my child?"

"I will," said Wally, and clung to the stony heart of her new father.

"Then stay with me and go no more among men; among them there is strife, with me there is peace."

"But Joseph, whom I love," said Wally, "shall I never have him?"

"Let him be," replied the mountain, "thou mayest not love him; he is a chamois hunter, and to such as he my daughters have sworn destruction. Come, I will take thee to them, that they may deaden thy heart, else thou canst not live in our eternal peace." And he carried her through wide halls and endless galleries of ice till they came to a vast hall that was transparent as though of crystal;

the rays of the sun shone through and broke into millions of coloured sparks, and through the walls heaven and earth gleamed in varied and mingled splendour.   There white maiden-forms, glistening like snow, with waving veils of mist, were playing with a herd of chamois, and it was charming to see them sporting with the swift-footed animals, catching them and chasing them here and there. These were Murzoll's daughters, the "phantom maidens" of the Oetz valley.   They crowded inquisitively round Wally as Murzoll set her down on the slippery glass of the floor.   They were as beautiful as angels, and had faces like milk and blood; but as Wally observed them more closely, a slight shudder ran through her, for she saw that they had all eyes of ice, like their father, and that the rosy hue of their cheeks and lips was not that of blood, but the sap of the Alpine rose, and they were as cold as frozen snow.

"Will you receive this maiden?" asked Murzoll. "I like her, she is strong and firm as the rock, she shall be your sister."

"She is fair," said the maidens; "she has eyes like the chamois. But she has warm blood, and she loves a hunter—we know!"

"Lay your hands on her heart that she may be

frozen with all her love, and live in bliss with you," said Murzoll.

The damsels hastened to her—it was like the breath of a snow storm—and laid their cold white hands on her heart; already she felt it shrink and throb more slowly. But she kept off the maidens with both arms and cried, "No, no, leave me. I want none of your bliss, I want only Joseph."

"If thou goest back amongst men we will dash Joseph to pieces, and throw thee and him into the abyss," threatened the phantom maidens; "for no one may live among men who has seen us."

"Throw me into the abyss, but leave me my heart to love. All, anything I will bear, but I will not part from my love," and with the strength of despair Wally seized one of the damsels round the waist and wrestled with her; and behold! the tender form was shattered in her arms, and she held in her hand only dripping snow. The daylight was extinguished; suddenly all was veiled in grey twilight. She stood on the bare rock; a sharp wind drove needles of ice in her face, and instead of the "phantom maidens" white mists whirled round her in a wild dance. High above, Murzoll's pale countenance looked darkly down upon her through the clouds, and his voice of thunder said,

"Dost thou rebel against Men and Gods?—

Heaven and earth will be thy enemies. Woe is thee!" And all had vanished—Wally awoke. The chill evening wind whistled through the window-slits on the girl. She rubbed her eyes; her heart still trembled at the weird dream; she thought long before she knew where she was, or could separate the images of her dream from the reality; an inexplicable sense of horror remained in her mind and mingled itself with all she saw. She rose from her bed and involuntarily called loudly for the servant. She went out of the hut to seek him; it was a clear and beautiful evening; the mists were scattered, but the sun was low and the breeze blew keenly from the heights. Wally hastened hither and thither in search of the deaf man; she found only the pile of firewood that he had made for her. Then it occurred to her that he had said he would go away while she was asleep. It was so; he had not waited for her awakening. It was not right of him to abandon her while she slept. To wake thus and find no one; it was hard! All was so silent around her, so deserted and empty. It must be six o'clock and milking time. The confiding cattle would look at the stable door, where no mistress would come in with bread and salt for them—she was sitting up here with her hands in her lap, and around her far and wide stirred no living thing. Oh! the deathly

stillness and inaction—she knew not how she felt—
alone, so terribly alone! She climbed higher still,
on to an overhanging point, that she might look
down upon the wide world. A vast unknown picture was spread before her eyes in the purple of
the setting sun. There lay before her to the very
verge of the horizon the great range of the Tyrol,
in the distance growing fainter and fainter, close
at hand crushing and overpowering her with their
great silent sublimity; between them, like children
in their father's arms, slept the blooming valleys.
A nameless longing seized her for the beloved fields
of home, that even now lay reposing peacefully
before her eyes in the evening shadows. The sun
had set, and on the horizon lay violet clouds shot
with streaks of ruddy gold; little by little, the pale
full moon began to shine, contesting the victory
with the last flickering gleams of day. Down in
the valleys it was already night; here and there,
scarcely visible in the distance, a light glimmered
from afar—a star of earth. Now they were going
to rest, her weary companions down yonder. With
them all was well; a friendly roof was above their
heads; they rested securely in the bosom of a
sheltered home—perhaps, already half-asleep, they
still listened behind the coloured curtain of the
little window to the beloved one's song—only she

was alone, thrust forth and banished, exposed defenceless to every terror, her only shelter the inhospitable hut, where the wind whistled through the empty window-slits. "Father, father, how could thou have the heart to do it?" she cried aloud, but near and far nothing answered but the rush of the night-wind. Higher and higher rose the moon, the streaks of light in the west lost their gold, and glimmered only a pale yellow in the darkness of the evening sky. The outlines of the mountains seemed to shift and grow larger in the twilight; threatening, overpowering, her nearest neighbour, the mighty Similaun, looked down upon her. All the giant peaks around seemed to stare at her frowningly, because she had dared to spy out their nightly aspect. It was as though only since Wally's arrival, they had all become so still and quiet—as a company that confers of private affairs is suddenly dumb when a stranger enters. There she stood, the helpless human form, so lonely in the midst of this silent, motionless world of ice, so inaccessibly high above all living things, so strange in the weird company of clouds and glaciers, in the terrible, mysterious silence. "Now art thou all alone in the world!" cried an inner voice, and an unspeakable anguish, the anguish of the forsaken ones, swept over her. It seemed to her all at once as though she were doomed to go on, for ever lost, through vast immeasurable space, and as though seeking help she clung to the steep wall of rock, pressing her wildly-beating heart against the cold stone.

What passed within her in that hour, she herself did not know, but it seemed as though the stone against which she pressed her young, warm, trembling heart, had exercised some mysterious power over her, for that hour left her hard and rough as if she had been in very truth Murzoll's child.

———

CHAPTER V.

Old Luckard.

WHEN about a week later the herdsman came
up the mountain with the flocks, Wally almost
frightened him, she looked so wasted away; but
when he said to her, "Thy father bids me ask thee
if thou'st had enough of being up here, and if
thou'll do thy duty?"—she set her teeth and answered, "Tell my father, I'd sooner let myself be
eaten piecemeal by the vultures, than do anything
to please them that drove me up here!"

This was for the present the last message that
passed between her and her father.

When Wally had her little flock around her,
which consisted only of sheep and goats, for larger
animals could not find sufficient food on these
heights, then her old spirit revived and the mountain
lost its terrors for her. In the midst of her helpless
charges she was no longer alone, she had again
some one to work for, something to care about.
For though the vulture had been a faithful companion, yet he could not do away with the in-
activity that had driven her almost to despair, and

allowed dark thoughts to gain the mastery over her.

So little by little she became accustomed to the solitude, and it grew dear and sweet to her. Life with its daily claims, small and great, narrows and confines every great nature: up here Wally's untameable spirit could expand without constraint; up here was freedom—no human being to gainsay her, no alien will to oppose itself to hers—and standing there, the only soul-gifted being far and wide, by degrees she felt herself a queen on her solitary, lofty throne, a sovereign in the unmeasurable, silent realm that lay beneath her eyes. And she looked down at last from her heights with a mixture of pity and scorn on the miserable race below, who, wrapped in earth-born clouds, spent their lives in longing and grasping, in haggling and hoarding, and a secret aversion took the place of her first home-sickness. There, far below, were strife and anguish and crime. Murzoll had spoken truly in her dream—up here among the pure elements of ice and snow, in the clear atmosphere, free from all smoke, or pestilential taint of death— here was peace, here was innocence; here among the mighty tranquil mountain forms, which in the beginning had terrified her, the sentiment of the sublime had flooded her soul and had raised it far

above the common measure of mankind. One only
of all those low earthly inhabitants remained to her
dear and beautiful and great as before. It was
Joseph the bear-slayer, the Saint George of her
dreams. But he, like herself, dwelt more on the
heights than in the valleys, he had climbed all the
sky-piercing peaks on which no other foot would
venture, he brought down the chamois from the
steepest rocks, and for him nor height nor depth
had any terror; he was the strongest, the bravest of
men, as she was the strongest, the bravest of
maidens. In all the Tyrol no maiden was worthy
of him but herself; in all the Tyrol no man was
worthy of her but he. They belonged to one another, they were the giants of the mountains; with
the puny race of the valleys they had nothing in
common.

So, in her solitude, she lived for him only, and
awaited the day when this promise should be fulfilled to her. That day must come, and being
certain of this, she did not lose patience.

Thus the summer passed away, and winter fell
upon the valleys, and soon Wally must descend
with its wild forerunners, the storm and the snow,
to her estranged home. She quailed at the thought.
Rather would she have crept up here into some
deepest ice-cave with suspended existence like the

wild bear than go down again to the noise and smoke of the low spinning-room, and be wedged, together with her morose father, her detested suitor, and the malicious servants, within the narrow compass of the house, imprisoned behind walls of snow a foot high, out of which, often for weeks at a time, no escape was possible.

The nearer the time came, the heavier her heart grew, the more despondingly did she revolt against the thought of that imprisonment; but time passed on, and no one came to fetch her; it seemed as though down there she was entirely forgotten. Colder ever and more wintry grew the weather, the days ever shorter, the nights ever longer; two sheep perished in a snow-storm; soon the animals could find no more food, and the time for fetching home the flocks was gone and past. "They mean to leave us to die up here of hunger," said Wally to the vulture, as she divided her last piece of cheese with him, and a secret horror swept over her; the young healthy life rebelled within her against the terrible thought. What should she do? Forsake the flock and find the homeward track, leaving the innocent beasts to perish miserably? Nay!—that Wally would not do—she would stand or fall like a brave commander with his troops. Or should she set out together with the flocks, all ignorant of the road as she was, and wander over the snow-covered Ferner to see at last one animal after another sink amid the ice and snow, or fall into the clefts of the rock? This also was impossible; she could do nothing but wait.

At last, one misty autumn morning when she could not see her hand before her face for the fog, when the little flock, trembling with frost, were all huddled together in their fold, and Wally, stiff with cold, sat over the fire on the hearth—then the boy appeared to conduct her home. And though she had shrunk with horror from the thought of slowly starving up here with her flock, yet now all her former dread of the return home came upon her again, and she knew not which seemed the greater evil—to sink here by the side of her harsh father Murzoll, or to be obliged to go back to her real father.

The herd-boy broke the silence: "Thy father bids me tell thee thou's not to come into his sight unless thou'll do as he bids thee; but, if thou'll not hear reason, then thou may stay with the cow-herd in the stable—into the house thou shall not come; that he's sworn." "So much the better," said Wally, drawing a deep breath, and the boy stared at her in astonishment.

Now she could go down with a light heart;

now she would be spared all contact with those hated people, and could live for herself in barn and stable; what her father had devised as a punishment, was to her an act of kindness. Now she could indulge her thoughts undisturbed; and if she was in need of encouragement there was old Luckard who was always so good to her. Yes, in her solitude she had first learned to understand what was the true worth of such a faithful heart, and that her father could not take from her.

She set to work almost cheerfully to prepare for her homeward journey; for now that her dread of the hateful intercourse with her father was removed, she could think with silent joy on the gladness of the old woman at the return of her foster-child. There was still some one down yonder who took pleasure in her, and that thought did her good.

"Come, Hansl," she said when all was packed to the vulture, who, with ruffled feathers, sat unwilling to move on the hearth, "now we are off to see old Luckard!"

"But Luckard's not at the farm any more," said the boy.

"Why, where is she, then?" asked Wally startled.

"The master has turned her out."

"Turned her out! old Luckard!" cried Wally. "Why, what's been the matter?"

"She couldn't get on with Vincenz, and he's everything with the master now," the boy explained in a tone of indifference, and, whistling, he hoisted the bundle of Wally's things. Wally had turned quite pale. "And where is she now?" she asked.

"With old Annemiedel in Winterstall."

"How long ago did it happen?"

"Oh, about three weeks ago. She cried ever so, and could hardly walk, the fright went to her knees; Klettenmaier and the boy had to hold her or she'd have tumbled down. All the village stood round and looked on to see her go away."

Wally had listened motionless, her sunburnt face had turned quite pale, and her breast heaved painfully. When the boy had ended, she seized her staff from the wall, flung the vulture on to her shoulder, and stepped out of the hut.

"Go on first," she commanded in a hoarse voice. The little flock was quickly assembled, the milking gear packed together, and the procession set itself in motion. Wally spoke not a word; a fearful tension marked her features, and with lips pressed together, a threatening line that recalled her father's look between her thick brows, she led the flock onwards with long strides, her firm step leaving deep tracks in the snow. Faster and ever faster she walked, the farther down she got, till the boy with

the flock could scarcely keep up with her, and where
the way was steep she struck the iron point of her
staff into the soil and swung herself down with a
mighty spring, so that only the vulture in the air
could follow her path over cliffs and crevasses.
Often both herdsman and flock vanished in the mist
behind her; then she stood still and waited a moment till they were in sight, and when the boy had
indicated the direction of the road, on she went
again without rest or pause, as if it were a matter
of life and death.

At last the region of perpetual snow was passed,
and at Wally's feet lay Vent, as it had lain six
months before when she had gone up the mountain;
only not now in the glow of the May sunshine, but
forlorn, autumnal, cold and dead. The boy an-
nounced that they must rest there for a while.
Wally refused, but the boy declared it would be as
good as killing both man and beast, not to rest for
half an hour.

"As thou will," said Wally, "stay—. I am going
on. If they ask where I am when thou gets
home, say only that I am gone to old Luckard."
And she strode on, the flapping wings of the faithful Hansl rustling over her; he could fly now as he
liked, for Wally no longer clipped his wings.

Now she had reached the spot where on her

upward journey Luckard had bid her farewell and
turned homewards again. "Dear old Luckard!"
Wally fancied she could see her again quite plainly,
crying in her apron as she turned away, waving her
one more farewell with her brown, bony arms, her
silver locks that always hung from below her cap
fluttering in the wind.   She had grown grey in
honour and fidelity in Stromminger's house, and
now shame had fallen on that white head!   And
Wally had parted from her so lightly, and repressed
her tears, and had torn herself impatiently away
when the old woman in her grief would not let her
go; and no foreboding had warned her of the fate
to which she was sending the unprotected old servant with that brief farewell, or that Luckard for
her sake would suffer hardship and disgrace. Wally
ran and ran as if she could overtake Luckard going
down the road as she had gone six months before;
and in spite of the autumn frost, the sweat stood
on her brow, the sweat of a winged haste to pay
her heavy debt of gratitude; and hot tears gathered
in her eyes as she seemed always to see the old
woman silently walking and walking on before her.
She went so slowly, poor old Luckard, and Wally
so fast; and yet they remained always as far apart,
and Wally could not overtake her.

For one instant must Wally pause for rest and

breath. She wiped the drops from her brow and the tears from her eyes; then she felt as if driven inexorably onwards again. "Wait, Luckard, only wait, I'm coming to thee," she murmured breathlessly to herself, as if for her own comfort.

At last the church tower of Heiligkreuz rose up before her, and from thence a giddy path led high over the torrent to a solitary group of houses on the farther side of the ravine. This was the little spot called Winterstall, where Luckard was living. Wally passed behind the houses of Heiligkreuz, and crossed the slight bridge beneath which the wild waters of the Ache roared and foamed as though they would sprinkle with their angry froth even the defiant girl who looked carelessly down into the awful depths as though neither danger nor dizziness existed in the world. The bridge was passed, still a steep bit of road remained, and then at last it was reached, the goal for which she had striven with a beating heart; she was in Winterstall, and there just to the left of the path stood the hut of Luckard's cousin, old Annemiedel, its tiny windows deep set beneath the overhanging thatch. Behind them, no doubt, the old woman sat spinning, as was her custom in the winter-season, and Wally drew a deep breath out of a lightened heart. She had reached the cottage, and before entering she looked smiling through the low window for Luckard. But there was no one in the room; it looked empty and deserted with an unmade bed in one corner left standing in a disorderly heap. Above it, a smoke-blackened wooden Christ stretched his arms on a cross, on which were hung a piece of crape and a dusty garland of rue. It was a dreary scene, and at the sight of it all joy forsook Wally; she set down the vulture on a rail, unlatched the door and stepped into the narrow passage. At one end an open door led into the little kitchen, where a small fire of brushwood smouldered on the hearth. Some one was there busily at work; it must certainly be old Luckard, and with a beating heart Wally walked in. The cousin stood on the hearth cutting up bread for her soup. No one else was there.

"Oh, my God! Wally Stromminger!" cried the old woman, and let her knife fall into the platter in her astonishment. "Oh, my God, what a pity, what a pity!"

"Where is Luckard?" said Wally.

"She is dead! Oh, my God, if thou'd only come three days sooner—we buried her yesterday." Wally leant silent and with closed eyes against the door post; no sign betrayed what was passing in her soul.

"It's a real pity!" continued the old woman

loquaciously. "Luckard said she felt as if she couldn't die without seeing thee once more, and thou was always coming on the cards, and day and night she would listen to hear if thou wasn't coming. And when she felt herself near death, 'After all, I must die,' she said, 'and I've never seen the child,' and then she would have the cards once more, and she wanted to lay them out for thee in the very death-struggle, but she couldn't do it, her hand shook on the counterpane. 'I can see no more,' she said, and lay back, and it was all over."

Wally clasped her hands over her face, but still no word passed her lips.

"Come into the bedroom," said the old woman goodnaturedly. "I've hardly borne to go in there since they carried Luckard out. I'm always so alone, and I was so glad when my cousin came and said now she'd stay with me. But I soon saw she couldn't live long after her disgrace. It went to her stomach, she could hardly eat anything, and every night I could hear her crying, and so she got always weaker and thinner—till she died."

The old woman had opened the door of the room into which Wally had looked before, and they went in. A swarm of autumn flies buzzed up. In the corner stood Luckard's old spinning wheel silent and still, and the empty disordered bed confronted it sadly.

From a panelled cupboard on which the black Virgin of Altenötting was depicted, Annemiedel took a worn pack of German cards.

"There, see; I laid the pack by for thee, I was sure thee would come. It always stood so on the cards. They're true witches' cards these, and a pack that has had the touch of a dead hand on it, that is doubly good. I don't know what misfortune they're sending thee, but Luckard always shook her head and read them with a fearful heart. She never told me what she saw in them, but for sure it was no good."

She gave Wally the cards; Wally took them in silence and put them in her pocket. The cousin wondered that Luckard's death should not touch her more nearly, that she should be so quiet and not even shed a tear.

"I must go," the old woman said, "I've got my soup on the fire. Say, thou'll dine with me?"

"Yes, yes," said Wally gloomily, "only go, cousin, and let me rest awhile. I sprang almost straight down here from the Hochjoch."

Annemiedel went away shaking her head. "If Luckard had only known what a hard-hearted thing it is!"

Scarcely was Wally alone when she bolted the door behind the old woman and fell on her knees by the empty bed. She drew the cards from her pocket, laid them before her, and folded her hands over them as over some holy relic.

"Oh! Oh!" she cried aloud, in a sudden outburst of grief: "Thou'st had to die, and I was not with thee; and in all my life long thou's always been loving and good to me—and I—I did not pay it back. Luckard, dear old Luckard, can thou not hear me? I am here now—and now it is too late. They left me up there. There's no herdsman they'd have left so long, and it was all malice, that I might just be frozen and then give in! It had already cost me two of my flock—and now thee too, thou poor good Luckard!"

Suddenly she sprang to her feet; her eyes red with crying flashed with a feverish light, she clenched her brown fists. "Only wait down yonder, you scoundrels—only wait till I come. I will teach you to drive innocent and helpless folk out of house and home. As true as God is above us, Luckard, thou shall hear even in thy grave how I will stand up for thee!"

Her eyes fell on the crucifix over the dead woman's bed. "And Thou! Thou let'st everything go as it will, and Thou helps no one that cannot help him-

self," she murmured bitterly in her storm of grief
to the silent enduring image above, whose signi-
ficance she never could understand.   She was terrible in her righteous anger.   All that lay in her
of her father's inflexible nature had developed itself
unfettered up yonder in the wilds, and her great
and noble heart that knew none but the purest im-
pulses drove without suspecting it ill-seething blood
through her veins.

She gathered together her sacred relics, the
cards, on which the dying woman's clammy fingers
had traced the last message of her love; then she
went out into the kitchen to Annemiedel.

"I will now go on, cousin," she said calmly, "I
only beg thee to tell me how things fell out between Luckard and Stromminger—" she no longer
called him father.   The old woman had just served
the soup in a wooden bowl and she insisted on
Wally's sharing it with her.

"Thou must know," she said, while Wally was
eating, "Vincenz there, he knows just how to come
over thy father, and he's got the better of him altogether.   Ever since the summer, Stromminger's had
a bad foot and cannot walk.   So Vincenz goes up
to him every evening and passes the time for him
playing cards, and always lets him win—he thinks
he'll gain once for all when he wins thee.   The

old man can hardly live now without Vincenz, and
so little by little he's given him the oversight of
everything, because with his lame foot he can never
get about himself. So Vincenz thinks now the
house and farm half belong to him already, and
bustles in and out just as he pleases. That was
how the quarrel began with Luckard, for Luckard,
she would always see that everything was right and
fair, as she was used to do, and Vincenz took everything out of her hands and she durst never say a
word. Then when he saw that Luckard was down-
right pining, he said to her that he'd let her manage
everything just as if she'd been mistress, and that
he'd take care to wink at anything she might like
to do, if she'd only help him to get thee—for he
knew very well that she could do anything with
thee. And then Luckard grew angry; 'She'd never
stolen in her life,' she said, 'and wasn't going to
begin now in her old age—she wanted nothing but
what she could earn honestly, and that as for the
man who'd look on at cheating and say nothing,
she'd never recommend him to Wally,' she said.
And what does the villain do? goes straight to
Stromminger and accuses Luckard. He'd convinced
himself now, he said, that it was only Luckard that
had set thee against him and thy father, and it was
all her doing, he said, that thou was so unruly, be-

cause she was fain to hold everything under her own hand. That's how it all came about. And it just broke her heart to think that such things were believed of her, when not a word of it all was true. It grieved her such injustice should be done. Is it not true, she never said to thee that thou shouldn't obey thy father?"

"Never, never; on the contrary she was always humble and discreet, and never talked about what she had nothing to do with," said Wally, and again her burning eyes were wet. She turned away her face and rose to go. "God keep thee, cousin," she said, "I'll soon come back again." She took her staff and hat, called her bird, and set out hastily towards home.

CHAPTER VI.

A Day at Home.

As Wally went back across the bridge, she turned giddy; she felt now for the first time how the blood had mounted to her head. The milder air down here that felt heavy and oppressive after the clear, icy atmosphere of the Ferner, the bird that clung tightly to her shoulder as her rapid movements made his hold insecure—all seemed painful, almost unbearable. At last she came to the village where her home stood, but to reach it she was obliged to go the whole length of the street, to the very last house. All the villagers, who had just finished their dinners, put their heads out of window and pointed at her with their fingers. "See, there goes the Vulture-maiden. Hast ventured down at last, then? And thou's brought the vulture back with thee, thou and he were not frozen together, then? Thy father left thee to shiver up there long enough!" "Let's see, now, how thou'rt looking? As brown and lean as a Schnalser herdsman." "He! he! thou's grown tame enough up yonder; yes, yes, that's the way to serve such as will not obey their father!"

A shower of spiteful comments such as these fell around Wally; she kept her eyes bent on the ground, and the burning red of shame and bitterness mounted to her brow. Insulted—scoffed at— thus the proud daughter of the chief peasant returned to her home. And all—for what? An implacable hatred rose up in her, sorer, bitterer than anger; for anger may subside, but the deep hatred that grows in an embittered, ill-treated heart strikes its roots through the whole being; it is the silent, persistent outcome of helpless revenge.

Silently Wally mounted the hill behind the hamlet whence Stromminger's farm looked proudly down. No one noticed her arrival but the deaf Klettenmaier, who was splitting wood for winter-use under the wooden shed in the yard; all the others were in the field.

"God be praised," he said, and took off his cap to his master's child. She set down her burden, the heavy vulture, on the ground, and gave her hand to the old man.

"Thou's heard?" he said. "Old Luckard?"

Wally nodded.

"Ay! ay!" he continued without interrupting his work. "If Vincenz once takes a dislike to any one he never rests till he's driven them out. He'd be glad enough to see me off the place, for he knows

very well I always held by Luckard, and he thinks
that if no one was left at the farm to help thee,
thou dursn't be so wilful. And because there's nothing else he can do to me, he leaves me always
the hardest work; I've a whole waggon load of
wood to cut up every day, but I can't do it for
long. See, I'm nearly seventy-six years old, and
this is the third day. But that's just what he wants,
to be able to tell Stromminger that I'm no longer
good for anything, or else for me to go away of
myself when I can hold out no more. But where
could I go—an old man like me? I *must* hold
out."

Wally had listened with a gloomy countenance
to the old man's speech. Now she went quickly
into the house to fetch bread and wine for him;
but the store-room was locked and so was the
cellar. Wally went into the kitchen. Her heart
felt a pang—here had been Luckard's peculiar
domain, and she felt as if the old woman *must*
come to meet her and ask: "How is it with thee?—
what does thou want?—what can I do to serve
thee?" But all that was over and gone. A strange
and sturdy servant girl sat on the hearth, peeling
potatoes.

"Where are the keys?" asked Wally.

"What keys?"

"The keys of the store-room and the cellar!"

The girl looked insolently at Wally. "Ho, ho! what next—and who may thou be?"

"That thou might guess well enough," said Wally proudly, "I am the master's daughter."

"Ha, ha," laughed the girl, "then thou may just take thyself out of the kitchen. The master has forbidden that thou should come into the house. Over there in the barn—that's thy place. Dost understand me?"

Wally grew pale as death. Thus, then—thus was she to be received in her father's house. Wallburga, daughter of the Strommingers, must give way to the lowest servant girl on the estate to which she was heir! Not only was she to be forbidden her father's presence—it was intended to break her spirit through degrading humiliations. She, Wally, the Vulture-maiden, of whom her father had once proudly said that a girl like her was worth ten boys!

"Give me the keys!" she commanded in a firm voice.

"Ha! ha! that's better still. The master has ordered us to look on thee as a stable girl—there's no question of keys there. I look after the house, and I give out nothing but what the master allows."

"The keys," cried Wally in an outburst of anger, "I command thee!"

"Thou's no call to command me—dost understand? I'm Stromminger's servant, and none of thine. And I am master in the kitchen, dost understand? It's Stromminger's orders. And if Stromminger holds his own daughter lower than a servant —no doubt he knows the reason why!"

Wally stepped close up to the servant, her eyes flashed, her lips quivered; the girl was frightened. But only for an instant did the struggle last in Wally, then her pride conquered; with the miserable serving maid she had nothing to do. She left the house. Her pulses beat like hammers, her eyes swam, her bosom rose and fell in gasps; it was too much — all that this day had brought her. She crossed the yard, took the cleaver from the hand of the old man who was trembling with his efforts, and led him to a bench that he might rest himself. He honestly resisted, he dared not leave his task incomplete; but Wally made him understand she would do his work for him.

"God bless thee, thou hast a good heart," said the man, seating himself wearily on the bench. Wally went into the shed and split the heavy logs with mighty blows. So wrathfully did she swing the axe that at each stroke she hit it through the wood deep into the block. The old man watched with astonishment how the work went on better in her hands than in a man's, and he took a pride in it—he had seen the child grow up from her birth and loved her in his own way. But Wally saw afar the hated form of Vincenz approaching, and involuntarily she discontinued her work. Vincenz did not see her. He came up from behind Klettenmaier, and suddenly stood close in front of the startled old man, whilst Wally observed him from within the shed. He seized the man by the doublet and pulled him up. "Hallo," he screamed in his ear, "dost call that working? thou lazy dawdle, thou; as often as I come by thou's sitting there doing nothing—now I've had enough of it—be off with thee," and he gave him a push with his knee, so that the trembling old man was flung to a distance on the stone pavement of the yard.

"Help, master! help me up," cried the man imploringly, but Vincenz had seized a cudgel and raised his arm. "Wait a bit—thou shall see how I help up a lazy knave!" he said. At this moment such a blow fell on Vincenz's head that he uttered a loud cry and staggered backwards. "God in heaven, what is that?" he stammered and sank upon the bench.

"It is the Vulture-maiden," answered a voice

trembling with rage, and Wally, the hatchet in her hand, stood before him with white lips and staring eyes, struggling for breath as if the wild pulses of her heart were choking her.

"Did thou feel that?" she panted out with breathless pauses. "Dost know now how it feels to get a heavy blow? I'll teach thee to oppress my faithful old servant. Thou'st already sent my Luckard underground, and now thou'll do the same by this old man? Nay, before I'll suffer such a deed, I'll set my whole inheritance in flames and smoke thee out of it as I would a fox." Meanwhile she had helped up old Klettenmaier, and led him out to the barn. "Go in, Klettenmaier," she said, "and recover thyself, *I* order thee."

Klettenmaier obeyed; he felt that at this moment she was master, but at the door he freed himself from her support and said, shaking his head, "Thou shouldn't have done it, Wally—go and look after Vincenz; I fear thou'st given him a heavy blow."

She left the old man and went out again. Vincenz lay quite still. Wally looked at him with half-averted eyes; he had lost consciousness and lay stretched out on the bench, and blood dripped from his head on to the ground. With quick decision, Wally went into the kitchen and called to the girl;

"Come out here; bring some vinegar and a cloth and help me."

"What, thou's more orders to give already," said the girl, laughing out loud, without stirring from the spot where she sat.

"It's not for me," said Wally with a dark and evil glance, as she took the vinegar flask from the shelf. "Vincenz is lying out there—I've half killed him."

"Heaven and earth!" shrieked the maid; and instead of hastening to help Vincenz, she ran screaming about the house and yard. "Help, help," she cried; "Wally has struck Vincenz dead!" And from every side the alarm cry was echoed back till it reached even to the village, and every one ran to the spot.

Wally had meanwhile called Klettenmaier to her assistance, and was washing the face of the senseless man with vinegar and water. She could not understand how it was the wound was so deep, for she had struck with the back of the hatchet, and not with the sharp edge; but the blow had been dealt with a force of which she herself was unconscious. Her long restrained rage had concentrated itself in that one stroke, which came crashing down as if she were still splitting the logs of wood.

"What's happened here?" roared a voice in Wally's ear, and her blood stood still—her father had dragged himself out on his crutches. "What's happened here?" repeated twenty or thirty voices, and the yard was filled with people.

Wally was silent.

A buzzing murmur arose all round her, every one pressed forward, touching and examining the lifeless man. "Is he dead?" "Will he die?" "How came it about?" "Did Wally do it?" was asked from one to another.

She stood there as though she neither heard nor saw, and laid a bandage on the wounded Vincenz. "Can thou not speak?" thundered her father. "What hast thou done, Wally?"

"You can see!" was the short reply.

"She owns to it," they all shrieked together. "Gracious Heaven, what insolence!" "Thou gallows-bird, thou!" cried Stromminger. "Is it so thou comes down again to thy home?"

At the word "home," Wally gave a short bitter laugh and fixed a piercing glance on her father.

"Laugh away," cried Stromminger; "I thought thou'd learn better up there, and now, scarce a quarter of an hour in the house, thou's already at mischief again."

"He moves," cried one of the women, "he's still alive."

"Carry him into the house and lay him on my bed," ordered Stromminger, making way by the kitchen door against which he was leaning. Two men raised Vincenz and carried him indoors.

"If only the doctor were here," lamented the women, following the sick man into the room.

"If only we had old Luckard, we should need no doctor," said some of them, "she knew what was good for everything."

"Let her be fetched," cried Stromminger, "tell her to come this instant."

Again Wally laughed. "Yes, truly, old Luckard," she said. "Thou'd be glad to have her back again now, Stromminger! Thou must seek her now in the churchyard!"

The people looked at each other in consternation. "Is she dead?" asked Stromminger.

"Yes, three days ago she died — died heart-broken because of what you did to her. See, Stromminger, it serves thee right, and if yon man dies because there is no one by who knows how to cure him, it serves him right too; so much as that he has well deserved of Luckard."

Now there arose a tumult—this was too bad. "After such a deed to talk like this, and say it served him right, instead of repenting it. Why, no one's life was safe! and Stromminger to stand by and let her talk like that and never say a word! there was a fine father for you!" So they talked together, while Wally, with folded arms, stood defiantly in the kitchen door looking at Stromminger, who, in spite of himself, was hard hit by her reproaches. Now however his wrath returned with double force, and raising himself on his crutch he cried to the crowd; "I'll show you what manner of father I am! seize her and bind her."

"Yes, yes," cried the people confusedly, "bind her, such a one should be under lock and bolt— before the justice she shall go, the murderess."

Wally uttered a dull cry at the word "murderess," and drew back into the kitchen. "Hold," cried Stromminger. "Before a justice my daughter shall never go; do you think I'll live to see the chief peasant's child taken off to prison? Do you know Stromminger no better than that? Do *I* need a court of justice to punish a wilful girl? Stromminger himself is man enough for that, and on my own ground and my own territory I am my own judge and justice. I'll soon show you who Stromminger is, though I am lame. Into the cellar she shall go, and there remain under lock and key, till her proud spirit is broken and she comes after me on her knees before you all. You have heard, all of you, and if I don't keep my word you may set me down a rascal."

"Merciful God, hast Thou forgotten judgment?" cried Wally. "No, father no! for God's sake don't lock me up! Turn me out, send me up the Murzoll to perish in the snow—I'll die of hunger—I'll die of cold—but under the open heavens. If you lock me up, harm will come of it!"

"Aha, thou'd like to be off again wandering round like a vagabond — that would please thee better? Not so; I've been too soft with thee. Thou'll stop under lock and key till thou asks pardon on thy knees of me and of Vincenz."

"Father, all that is no good with me; sooner than do that, I'd rot away in the cellar—that you might know of yourself. Let me go, father, or, I tell you once more, harm will come of it."

"There—enough said. Well, you—what are you all standing there for? Are you dreaming? Am I to run after her with my lame foot? Seize her, but hold her fast—she has Stromminger blood in her that'll try your teeth—hold on there!"

The peasants, stung by this mockery, crowded into the kitchen. "We'll soon get hold of her!" they said scoffingly.

But with one spring Wally was at the hearth,

and had snatched burning brands from the fire. "The first that touches me, I'll singe him, hair and skin!" she cried, and stood like the archangel with the flaming sword.

All fell back.

"Shame upon you!" cried Stromminger. "All of you together might be a match for a girl! Strike the brands from her hand with a stick," he ordered, in a paroxysm of rage, for it was now a point of honour with him to master his daughter before the eyes of the whole village. Some of them ran and fetched sticks; it was like hunting a wild animal, and a wild animal Wally had in truth become. Her eyes bloodshot, the sweat of agony on her brow, her white teeth clenched, she defended herself against this pack of hounds, fought like the wild beast of the forest, without reflection, without calculation, for her freedom—her life's element. Now they struck with the sticks at the brands in her grasp, her only weapon, and she flung them into the midst of the crowd, so that they fell back on one another, shrieking; then, snatching another brand from the hearth, and yet another, she threw them like fiery shot at the heads of her assailants. The uproar grew louder.

"Water here," cried Stromminger, "fetch water, —put out the fire!"

This would be an end to everything; the fire once out, Wally was lost. One moment more, and the water would be brought—despair seized the girl. All at once there came a thought—a terrible, desperate thought; but there was no time for consideration; the thought was a deed before she could reflect upon it, and waving a burning log in her hand, she rushed swift as an arrow through her pursuers out into the courtyard, and hurled the brand with a mighty fling on to the hay-loft, right into the middle of the hay and straw.

There was a scream of terror and amazement. "Now put the fire out," cried Wally, and flew across the courtyard through the gate, away and away, whilst all in the farm hurried shouting and storming to extinguish the flames that were already blazing upwards through the roof.

With the rising pillar of smoke, as if born of the roaring flame, a dark object rose screeching from the roof, circled two or three times high overhead in the air, and then took flight in the direction in which Wally had fled.

Wally heard the rushing sound behind her; she thought it was her pursuers, and ran blindly on. It was already night, but there was no darkness, a clear light quivered all around her, so that she might still be seen from afar. She mounted a steep point of rock whence she could look down the road, and now she saw that her pursuer was coming through the air. She had attained her end, no one thought any more of following her. To save the farm buildings was a more pressing need, and all hands were engaged in the work. The vulture overtook her as she stood there, and bounded against her with such force as nearly to throw her down from the rock. She pressed the bird to her bosom and sank exhausted on the ground. With dazed eyes she looked up at the glare of the fire that shone afar, and lighted up the dark mountain tops around. With a glowing and angry aspect her deed looked down on her—threatening, wrathful, overpowering. From every church tower in the canton round sounded the dismal peal of warning, and the bells rang out quite distinctly, "Incendiary, incendiary." But the terrible song lulled her senses to sleep—unconsciousness dropped a kindly veil over her hunted spirit.

CHAPTER VII.

"Hard Wood."

DEEP night surrounded Wally when she once more opened her eyes. The red glow was extinguished, the bells were silent; far below her in the ravine the Ache thundered its monotone, and over her head high in the heavens, stood a star. She gazed at it as she lay motionless with upturned face on the ground, and it seemed to beam down upon her with a look of forgiveness. A wonderful sense of consolation breathed through the night. The wind caressingly cooled her burning brow, she sat up and began to collect her thoughts. It could not be late, the moon was not yet up, and the fire must have been very quickly extinguished. It must have been—for how could the conflagration spread when every one was there, and ready that moment to lend a helping hand? She knew not how it was, she searched herself to the very bottom of her soul, and she could not feel herself guilty. She had done it only from necessity, to keep off her pursuers whilst she gave them something else to do. She knew quite well that she would now be called an "incendiary," but was she one indeed? She raised her eyes to the stars over her head; it was as if now, for the first time, she held communion with the great God, and what He said to her was —forgiveness. The pure night-sky looked peacefully down on her, that open sky, for the love of which she had done the deed. Only under this high, vaulted dome of stars could she find space to breathe; to lie imprisoned in the gloomy cellar without light, without air, for weeks, for months— till, to escape, she went to the home of her hated suitor, and made herself a mockery and disgrace by open repentance on her knees before her father! It was worse than death—it was an impossibility!

The girl who in utter loneliness had for six long months been the guest of the inhospitable wilderness of the Ferner, who had watched through many nights with the storm, the hail, the rain for her wild associates; whose brow the fire of heaven had kissed before it quivered to earth; round whom the thunder had warred in all its terror, whilst its power was as yet unspent by the winds; the girl who had almost daily staked her life springing over some bottomless abyss to save a straying goat— this girl could no longer bend herself to the ideas and the tyranny of small minds, could not submit to bit and bridle like an animal, must defend her-

self for life—unto death. Men had no longer any
right over her; she had renounced them and mated
herself with the elements. What wonder that she
had called one of her wild companions—Fire—to
her aid when warring against man?

She could not understand it all, she had never
learnt to reflect about her own consciousness; she
knew not the "wherefore!" But she felt that God
would not call her to account, that He from His
supreme throne measured with a quite other stan-
dard than that of man; even to her, up on her
mountain heights, everything had appeared so small
that down in the valley she had thought so large—
how much more to Him up there in Heaven? God
alone understood her; down below they might think
her a criminal—God acquitted her.

She raised herself and shook the burden from
her soul, and felt herself as heretofore, vigorous and
confident, strong and free.

"Now, Hansl, what shall we do next?" asked
she of the vulture, to whom in her solitude she
had accustomed herself to talk aloud. Hansl was
at that moment watching some reptile of the night,
then snatched at it, and killed it.

"Thou'rt in the right," said Wally, "we must
seek our bread. For thee, it is well, thou can find
it anywhere—but I?" Suddenly the bird became

uneasy, flew up and watched something in the distance.

Then it occurred to Wally that as soon as the fire was out she would be searched for, and that she must get farther away as quickly as might be. But whither? Her first thought was Sölden. But the blood mounted to her face—might not Joseph think that she was running after him? And should he see her in disgrace and dishonour, poor, a runaway from home—pointed at and decried as an "incendiary."

No, he at least should never see her thus, rather would she run to the very ends of the earth. And without any further consideration she took the vulture on her shoulder—the only good or chattel that troubled her—and set out in the direction whence she had come in the morning, to Heiligkreuz.

She had walked for two hours, her feet were sore, she was weary to death, when the tower of Heiligkreuz rose up before her in the darkness, and, like a gleam from a lighthouse, the rising moon shone through the open belfry and showed the way to the aimless wanderer.

Stumbling with fatigue, she dragged herself through the sleeping village up to the church. Now and then a dog barked, as with quiet steps she

passed along. Whoever observed her now would
take her for a thief; she trembled as though she
really were one; to what had the proud Wally
Stromminger come!

Behind the church was the parsonage; near the
door was a wooden bench, and from wooden boxes
in the little windows bushes of withered mountain-
pinks hung down. Here she would remain till daylight; the priest would at least protect her from
ill-usage. She lay down on the bench, the vulture
perched on the railing at her head, and in a few
minutes nature asserted its rights and she was
asleep.

"May the Lord defend us! what foundling has
He sent me here!" sounded in Wally's ears, and
she opened her eyes. It was broad daylight, and
there stood by her none other than the reverend
curé himself.

"Praised be Christ the Lord," stammered Wally
in bewilderment, and put her feet down from the
bench.

"For ever and ever, Amen. My child, how did
you come here? who are you, and what strange
companion is that you have with you? it is almost
enough to frighten one!" said the priest with a
friendly smile.

"Your reverence," said Wally simply, "I've

something heavy on my conscience, and I would be glad to confess to you. My name is Wallburga, and I belong to Stromminger, the chief-peasant of the Sonnenplatte. I've run away from home; you see—Vincenz Gellner wanted to marry me, and I struck his head open with a blow, and then I set fire to my father's barn—"

The priest clasped his hands together. "God help us, what tales are these! So young, and so wicked already!"

"Your reverence, I am not really wicked, truly I am not—I wouldn't hurt a fly—but they made me do it!" said Wally, and she looked up at the priest with her large honest eyes, so that he was obliged to believe her whether he would or not.

"Come in," he said, "and tell me all about it— but leave that monster outside;" he meant the vulture. Wally flung the bird upwards into the air, so that it flew on to the roof; then she followed the priest into the little house, and he made her come into his sitting-room.

There all was still and peaceful. In the alcove stood a rough wooden bedstead with two flaming hearts painted over it, which to the curé signified the hearts of our Saviour and the Virgin Mary; over the bed was a holy-water cup in porcelain, and a shelf full of books of devotion; in the room there were more shelves with other books and an old writing desk, a brown bench behind a large heavy table, some wooden seats, a praying-stool beneath a great crucifix with a garland of edelweiss, and a few gaily coloured lithographs of the Pope and of various saints. From the ceiling hung a bird-cage with a crossbeak. An antique commode with lions'-heads holding rings in their mouths as handles to the heavy drawers, represented the luxury of the dwelling, and on this commode were all sorts of beautiful things. A little shrine with a carved saint, a glass box with a wax image of the infant Christ in a red silk cradle, a glass spinning wheel, and a bunch of tarnished artificial flowers, such as are made in convents, in a yellow vase under a glass shade; a small box with many coloured shells, a tiny model of a mine in a bottle, and, as a centre-piece, a little manger made in moss and sparkling fragments of spar, with delicately carved figures of men and beasts. A few pretty cups and mugs were not wanting amid these holy surroundings, and two small crystal salt cellars to the right and left of the nativity set off on either hand the central piece.

And all was as clean as if no such thing as dirt existed in the world. This commode with the various objects upon it constituted the child-like altar which the lonely priest, six thousand feet above the sea and above modern culture, had raised to the God of beauty. Here he had stood many a time when the snow was whirling outside and the storm rocked the little wooden house, and gazed musingly at the tiny, neatly-carved world within, shaking his head with a smile and saying, "What will not men do next?"

Much the same, thought Wally in passing by, as her glance fell on the marvellous trifles. Rich as her father was, such things as these had never found their way into his house; what indeed could the clumsy peasant have done with them? In her whole life she had never seen such things—she to whom, in comparison with her scythe and hay-fork, a spinning-wheel seemed the height of elegance. She felt as if in this little room she dare not move for fear of injuring something, as if here she must be particularly well-behaved. She wished to leave her iron-shod shoes at the door, so as not to spoil the smooth, white-scoured boards; but the priest would not allow it, so she trod as softly as she could and seated herself modestly at the farthest end of the bench which the curé offered her. The priest let his clear friendly eyes rest observingly upon her, and saw that she could not remove her astonished gaze from the ornaments on the

commode. The old man was a student of humanity.

"You would like first to look at my pretty little
things? Do so, my child; besides, you are not
just yet collected enough for the serious matters we
must speak of."

And he led Wally to the mysterious commode,
and explained everything to her, and told her where
each thing had come from.

Wally did not venture to speak, and looked and
listened full of reverence. When they had come to
the manger, the last and the best, "See," said the
priest, "here at the back is Jerusalem, and there
are the three Wise Kings who travelled to see the
Holy Child—see, there is the star that is guiding
them—and there lies the child in the manger, and
does not dream yet that he is born to suffer for
the sins of the whole world. For as yet He cannot
think, and has brought no remembrance with him
of His Heavenly home; for the Son of God became
in all things a real child of man, like any other—
else men might have said that there was no miracle
in being as good and patient as Jesus Christ was,
if He was the Son of God and had the power of God,
and that it was no use to strive to follow such an
example, if one was only an ordinary man. They say
it often enough as it is, and go on in their sins."

Wally looked at the pretty naked infant with his gold paper glory lying there so patiently, and when she thought of the stern dark crucified God as a poor helpless baby born to suffering, it touched her compassion, and she was sorry that she had been "so rude" to the poor crucified Being yesterday when standing by Luckard's bed.

"But why did He let it all happen to Him?" she said involuntarily more to herself than to the priest.

"Because He wanted to show mankind that they should not repay evil for evil, and should not revenge themselves; for God has said, 'Vengeance is mine.'" Wally grew red, and cast down her eyes.

"Now come, my child," said the wise man, "and make your confession."

"That will soon be done, your reverence," said Wally. And honest as was her nature, she related to him, in low and timid tones indeed but without any attempts at palliation, how all had happened, and soon the whole circumstances were made clear to the confessor. A mighty picture of life lay unrolled before him, sketched in rude and rough outlines, and he pitied the noble young blood that had grown wild between rugged rocks and rugged men.

Long after Wally had ended he sat silent, looking meditatively before him. His gaze fixed itself
on an old, much-read volume on a book-stand by
the wall; a stranger whom he had received hos-
pitably had given it to him; on the back stood
printed in gold letters—Das Niebelungen-Lied.

"Your reverence," said Wally, who took the
thoughtfulness on his features for an expression of
reproof; "it was too much, all coming together. I
was still full of anger about poor old Luckard, and
then he must needs strike the old man also. I
couldn't look on and see the old man beaten, that
I could not, and if it were all to come over again,
I should do just the same. An incendiary I am
not—not even though they call me one. When a
house is set fire to in broad daylight when everyone is about, nothing much can be burnt, that is
certain. I didn't know how else to help myself,
and I thought that if they had to put it out, they
couldn't come after me. And if that is a sin, then
I don't know what is to be done in this world
where men are so wicked and do one all the harm
they can."

"We must do as Christ did—suffer and endure!"
said the priest.

"But, your reverence," said Wally, "when Jesus
Christ let men do as they would with Him, He

knew *why* He did it—He wanted to teach people something. But I don't know why I should do it, for no one would learn anything of me in all the Oetz valley. And if I had let myself be locked up in the cellar ever so patiently, it would all have been for nothing, for nobody would have taken example by me, and it would very likely have cost me my life."

For a moment the priest paused to reflect; then he fixed his kindly observant eyes on Wally and shook his head.

"You wilful child, you. Even now you would like to begin some fresh dispute with me. They have wickedly roused and irritated you, till you imagine enmity and contradiction everywhere. Look round, recollect yourself and see where you are— you are with a servant of God, and God says 'I am Love.' And this shall be no empty word to you, I will show you that it is true. I will tell you that when all men hate and condemn you, still the good God loves you and forgives you. Such as you are, hard men, stern mountains, and wild storms have made you; and that the good God knows very well, for He can look into your heart and see that it is good and upright, however much you have been in fault. And He knows that no garden-flower can bloom in the desert, and that a rude axe never carved a fine image. But now look farther. If our Lord and Master finds a piece of rude carving in particularly good wood, so that it seems to Him worth the trouble of making something better out of it, then He Himself takes the knife and carves the bungling work of man, that under His hand it may grow into beauty. Now listen, for I say take heed not to let your heart grow harder, for when the Lord has cut once or twice at the wood, if He finds it too hard He grudges the trouble, and throws the work away. Take heed then, my child, that your heart be soft and yielding under the shaping finger of God. If its hard pressure seems to you unbearable, yield, and think you feel the hand of God that is working on you. And if pain cuts sharply into your soul, think it is the knife of God cutting away its ruggedness. Do you understand me?"

Wally nodded somewhat doubtfully.

"Well," said the old man, "I will make it still clearer to you. Which would you rather be, a rough stick with which men may perhaps fight and kill each other, and which when it is rotten is broken up and burnt, or a finely carved holy image like that one yonder that is set in a frame and devoutly honoured?"

This time Wally understood and nodded

quickly. "Why, of course—rather a holy image like that."

"Well, see now. Rude hands have made a rough block out of you, but God's hand can carve you into a holy image if you will do just as He bids you."

Wally looked at the speaker with wide, astonished eyes; she felt so strangely—pleased and yet ready to weep. After a long silence, she said timidly, "I don't know how it is, Sir, but with you everything is quite different to what it is anywhere else. No one ever spoke so to me before. The priest at Sölden always scolded and talked about the Devil and our sins; and I never knew what he would have, for at that time I had done nothing wrong. But you speak so that one can understand you—I mean that if I might stay with you—that would be the best for me; I'd work night and day and earn my bit of bread."

The curé considered a long time; then he shook his head mournfully.

"That cannot be, my poor child. Even if I myself wished it, it would not do. Though I might grant it to you in God's name, before men I dare not. For God sees the motive, men see only the deed. The priest in the confessional is one thing — the priest in common life is another. In the confessional he is the medium of Grace, in the world he is the medium of Law. He must incite men, by word and example, to honour and keep the law. Think what people would say if the priest took a notorious incendiary into his house. Would they understand why I did so? Never— they would only conclude that I had taken the sinner under my protection, and thereupon sin the more. And if afterwards we lived to see a really wicked incendiarism, I should have to reproach myself bitterly that I had given encouragement to it by my indulgence to you. Can you not under- stand this, and take it without murmuring as the unavoidable result of your deeds?"

"Yes," said Wally gloomily; and her eyes red- dened with repressed tears. Then she rose quickly and said shortly, "I thank your reverence very much then, and wish you good morning."

"Hey, hey," cried the priest, "so high-flown again already? Don't you think it will be shorter to go through the wall than through the door? In your place, I would sooner go straight through the wall!"

Wally stood still ashamed, and looked down at the floor. The old gentleman looked at her with a comical expression of wonder, "How much will it not cost you to subdue that hasty blood? Is that the way you mean to run off? Did I say I would leave you to your fate because I cannot keep you with me in my house? First of all, you must have breakfast with me, for man must eat, and God knows how long it is since you eat last. Then we will talk farther." He went to a sliding panel that opened into the kitchen, and called to the old maid-servant to get breakfast for three; then sitting down at his simple desk, he wrote down for Wally the names of a few peasants whom he knew to be worthy people.

"See, here is a whole list of honest men and women in the Oetz and Gurgler valleys," said he to Wally. "Try to find a place with one of them; over the mountain nothing will be yet known of your fault, and by the time people hear of it you can have shown yourself to be an honest girl, so that they will be willing to shut their eyes to it. You must not appeal to me, but you are as tall and as strong as a man, and they will gladly take you; you can work with a will and make yourself useful, if you choose. But you must learn to obey —must give in to custom and order, else you will do no good. I do not ask you to go back to your father, and let yourself be locked up in the cellar; that would be undue punishment, and do you more harm than good. Nor do I ask you to marry Vin-

cenz out of obedience to your father and make
yourself miserable for life. But I do ask of you
that you should curb your wild spirit in the service
of worthy people, in reasonable and regular activity,
and so become again a useful member of human
society. Will you promise me this?"

"I will try," said Wally, in her unwavering
honesty.

"That is all I ask of you in the first instance,
for I know well that you cannot with a good conscience promise more. But try to do it with an
honest will, and remember always that God throws
away wood that is too hard. I will go to-day to your
father and speak to his conscience, that he may
forgive you and be reconciled to you, or at least
not pursue you any farther. Give me news soon
of where you are, that I may let you know how
things stand."

Marianne brought the breakfast, and the pastor
said the morning prayers. Wally, too, devoutly
folded her hands, and from her deepest soul prayed
God that he would help her to become good and
useful; she was in such holy earnest—she would so
gladly have been good and useful, if only she had
known how.

When prayers were over, all three sat down, she,
and the pastor, and Marianne to breakfast. But

scarcely had they begun when a shout was heard outside. "A vulture! See, up on the roof there, a vulture! shoot him down, bring guns!"

"Heavens! my Hansl," cried Wally springing up, and would have run out at the door.

"Stop," cried the priest, "what are you doing? Why risk yourself needlessly? You cannot go out now, when at any moment your father's people may come to take you!"

"I'll not leave my Hansl in the lurch, come what may," cried Wally, and with one spring she stood outside the house.

The curé followed her, shaking his head. "The vulture is tame," she cried to the people. "He belongs to me; leave him alone."

"One can't leave a creature like that to fly about as it will," said the people, grumbling.

"Has he taken a sheep or a child?" asked Wally defiantly.

"No."

"Well, then, leave me and my bird unmolested!" said the girl; and she stood there with an air so proud and threatening that the people looked at her with astonishment. "Wally, Wally," gently warned the priest, "think of the hard wood."

"I do think, your reverence!" she said, and beckoned with her hand to the vulture. "Hansl, come back." The bird shot down from the roof, so that the people all shrank back frightened. She took him on her shoulder, and stepped up to the priest. "God keep your reverence," she said gently, "and thank you for all your kindness."

"Will you not come in and finish breakfast?" said the old man.

"No, I'll not leave the bird alone again, and besides I must go on—what have I to stay for?"

"May God and all the Saints preserve thee, then!" said the pastor troubled, while Marianne was furtively thrusting some food into the pocket of her pleated gown.

For a moment her foot lingered on the threshold that had grown dear to her, then she silently stepped forward between the people, who made way for her.

"Who is she?" they asked each other.

"She is a witch!" she heard them whisper behind her.

"She is a stranger," said the priest, "who came to make her confession to me."

CHAPTER VIII.

The Klötz Family of Rofen.

DAY after day Wally wandered round the canton
seeking a place, but no one would take her with
her vulture, and from him she would not part. Even
if she had abandoned him, he would have flown
back to her again, and as to killing the faithful
bird, such a thought could not enter her mind, let
what might befal her.   Now, in very truth, she was
the Vulture-maiden, for her destiny was inseparably
linked to that of the bird, and he had as much influence over it as a human being.   Luckard's old
cousin, to whom she once paid a passing visit,
would have taken her in gladly, but she would have
been too near home, and wholly in her father's
power.   She must go farther—as far as her feet
would carry her.   Every day the season grew more
severe; it began to snow, and the nights, which
Wally was often forced to spend in an open barn,
were keenly cold.   The clothes she wore grew old
and shabby, she began to look like a beggar and a
vagabond, and she was every day more summarily
dismissed from the doors where she ventured to

knock with her companion. She looked so strange that no good housewife now would let her work in the house for even a few hours, and eat at her table afterwards. They gave her a piece of bread at the door for "God's pity's sake;" and Wally, the haughty Wally, daughter of the Strommingers, sat down on the threshold and eat it. For she would not die! Life—tormented, baited, poor and naked —life was still fair to her, so long as she could hope that sooner or later Joseph might come to love her; for the sake of that hope she would bear every-thing—hunger, cold, weariness. But her frame, hitherto so powerful, began to fail under the con-stant consuming anxiety and tension, her eyes were dim, her feet refused to serve her, and as soon as she lay down quietly her thoughts whirled in her brain, and she fell into a feverish dose. With overwhelming dread she met the feeling that she might be going to fall ill. It was too much! If she were to lose consciousness in some barn or shed, she might be taken back to her father, she would find herself once more in his power. She had wandered up into the Gurgler valley, and as she had there found nothing to do, she had taken the weary road again over to the Oetz valley; she had been as far as Vent, which lying in the domain of her father Murzoll, seemed to her almost like a home. But there things had gone worse than ever with her; the ruder the place, the ruder the inhabitants, and when Wally arrived there, she found that the news of her deed had hastened to precede her, and that wherever she showed herself she was met with horror and aversion. She did not appeal to the curé of Heiligkreuz; he had desired her not, and she perceived that he had been right to do so; but for that reason she sought no more priests; not one of them would dare to take any interest in her.

The last door in Vent had just been closed upon her. Before her lay nothing but the cloud-reaching wall of the Platteykogel, the Wildspitz, and the Hochvernagtferner, which closed in the valley, and over which no pathway led. Here on all sides the world was shut in like a *cul-de-sac*, and she was at the end of it; she stood still and looked up and around at the steep and towering walls. It was a grey morning; thick snow had fallen during the night and lay all over the valley, which looked like a prodigious trough of snow; every trace of a path was obliterated. She sat down and thought, "If I go to sleep, and am frozen, it is an easy death." But it was not yet cold enough for that; the snow melted under her, and she was soon shivering from the wet. Then she started up and dragged herself up the slope that leads up behind Vent to the Hochjoch; from thence she could look over all the surrounding country, and here she became aware of a sort of furrow in the snow that led behind the village along by the Thalleitspitz into the very heart of the Ferner. It might be a footpath—but whither did it lead? She went up higher to get a wider view, and a bandage seemed to fall from her eyes —that was the path that led from Vent to Rofen— Rofen, the highest inhabited spot in the whole Tyrol, the last in the Oetz valley where men, like eagles, can still dwell, and of them only two families, the Klotz family and the Gestreins; Rofen that lies silent and hidden at the foot of the terrible Vernagt-glacier, on the shore of the lake of ice where no straying foot wanders from year's end to year's end, which a venerable tradition wraps in a mysterious veil. This was the place that Wally must strive to reach, this was the last refuge where she might per- haps find help, or at least could die in peace and unseen, like the wild animal of the desert. Thither would she go—to the Klötze of Rofen; they were the most renowned guides in all the Tyrol, they were at home on the mountains as the mountain-spirits themselves; they would understand how Wally would sooner burn down a house, would sooner die, than let herself be deprived of the breath of freedom;

and they could protect her against all the world, for the farms of Rofen had right of sanctuary. Duke Frederick had granted it in token of gratitude, because he once in sore distress had found refuge there from his enemies. Joseph the Second had indeed withdrawn it at the end of the last century, but the peasant clings to old usages, and the villagers of the Oetz valley willingly continued to hold it in honour. No one who sought and found asylum at Rofen could be touched; for the Rofeners—the Klötze and the Gestreins—harboured no one who did not deserve it, and were held in as great respect as their forefathers. An assault on their home-right would have been simply a sacrilege.

Wally lifted her arms to Heaven in passionate thankfulness to God who had shown her this path. Her head swimming, her feet stumbling, she strove for the last goal that her strength might yet avail to reach; first, downwards to the path that led from Vent, then again steeply upwards. For an endless hour she mounted the encumbered path; there they lay before her as if sleeping in the snow, the peaceful, honoured farms of Rofen, which she had so often seen from Murzoll looking like eagles' nests clinging to the cliff. Her heart beat so that she could hear it, her knees almost failed her; if she were to be turned away, even here! A fresh storm

8*

of snow whirled silently around her, and wrapped the whole scene in a white, shifting veil. It flitted and glanced before her eyes, and the white veil waved coldly about her head, but it melted on her fevered brow and flowed in drops down her face and hair, and she trembled again with the chill. At last she stood before the door of Nicodemus Klotz, and took hold of the iron knocker; but as she put out her hand, a strange light flashed before her eyes, she fell heavily against the door, then sank down in a heap on the ground.

On and on the white flakes drifted up the narrow valley and wrapped it in a shrouding veil, and heaped themselves before the well-closed door of Nicodemus Klotz over the stiffened body that lay there, till it was a peaceful white hillock.

Nicodemus Klotz sat on his warm bench by the stove, smoked his pipe, and looked comfortably out of window at the snow. So the peaceful half-hours passed by, whilst his brother Leander, a fine-looking hunter, read the weekly news out of a shabby paper. "It is coming down finely," said Nicodemus, blowing out a cloud of smoke.

"Yes," said Leander, looking up at the snow-flakes floating and swarming before the little window. Suddenly in the midst of the white whirl a dark wing struck on the panes, something fluttered and croaked, then flew up to the roof.

"There is something there," said Leander standing up.

"What matter?" growled the elder brother, "whatever it may have been, thou can't go out in this storm."

"Why not?" said Leander taking his rifle from the wall; the wing-stroke of the passing bird had roused his hunter's instincts; he must see what it was. He went to the door and opened it cautiously, so as not to disturb the bird by any noise. A mass of snow fell inwards, and he perceived the heap that had piled itself up on the threshold. He could not get out; he must fetch a spade to clear away the wall, and impatiently putting aside his gun, he began to shovel.

"Heavens! what is this?" he cried out suddenly, "Nicodemus, come—quick—here is some one buried under the snow—help me!"

His brother hastened forward; in a moment the heap was dug into, and a beautiful rounded arm appeared, and then from beneath the light covering, they drew forth a lifeless body.

"Good God! a maiden—and what a maiden!" whispered Leander as the beautiful head and the finely-moulded form revealed themselves.

"How can she have wandered up here?" said Nicodemus, shaking his head as he lifted, not without effort, the heavy body out of the snow.

"Is she dead?" asked Leander touching her, while his eyes rested with mingled alarm and pleasure on the pale, sunburnt face.

"She must instantly be rubbed," ordered Nicodemus, "inside, in the bedroom there."

They carried the weighty burthen into the house and laid it on Nicodemus' bed. "She must have lain a good half-hour out there; it must be about that time since I heard a heavy blow against the door, but I thought it was a lump of snow fallen from the roof."

Leander fetched a tub full of snow, and officiously tried to help in pulling off the girl's garments. "Let be," said the older and more discreet man, "that will not do—a youngster like thee; the girl'd be ashamed if she knew it. Do thou go out and see if thou can bring down one of the Gestreins, Kathrine or Marianne. Go!"

Leander could not take his eyes from the lifeless form. "Such a beautiful maid!" he muttered compassionately as he went out.

With gentle care the experienced man now undressed the girl, and rubbed her hard with the snow till warmth revived in her skin, and the blood began to circulate again. Then he dried her well, covered her up carefully, and poured a few drops of a strong cordial extracted from herbs down her throat. At last she recovered consciousness, turned and stretched herself, and looked once round the room; but her eyes were glazed and vacant, and muttering a few unintelligible words, she closed them again.

"She is ill," said Nicodemus to Leander, who at this moment reappeared, whilst a sturdy peasant woman who stopped at the door to shake off the snow followed him.

"Marianne," said Nicodemus—she was his married sister, "thou must help us here. Two men like Leander and me can't look after the girl. There is Leander making eyes at her already."

He threw a dissatisfied glance at the young man, who was again standing by the head of the bed and seemed to devour with his eyes the face of the sick girl; but he turned away hastily and blushed at being found out.

Marianne went up to the bed, and her first question was: "Who can she be?"

"God only knows! Some vagabond," said Nicodemus.

"What should make thee say that?" growled Leander, "one can see plainly enough she's no vagabond."

"Ay, because she's a handsome girl and pleases thee," said Marianne; "there's many a fair face covers a blackened soul—good looks prove nothing; a decent girl doesn't wander round the country at this time of year, all alone in the snow till she falls in a heap. Likely enough she's in some scrape, and God knows what sort she may be to harbour in the house."

"Well, it's all one now," said Nicodemus good-naturedly, "we can't turn a sick girl out in the cold and snow, be she what she may."

"As you will," said the woman, "I'll come over here and welcome, to take care of her for you; but I won't take her into my house, and that you may know once for all."

"No one asked thee; we will keep her ourselves," said Leander irritated, and as Wally again muttered some words to herself, he leaned tenderly over her and asked, "What is it? What dost thou want?"

The elder brother and sister exchanged glances. "As for thee," said Nicodemus, "I have something to say to thee. Thou's willing enough and ready to open house and home before we know who this woman is. There stands the door;—now walk out and come in here no more unless thou'd like to see me turn out the girl, ill as she is. Dost understand?"

"What, one mayn't even look at a girl now," grumbled Leander, "I see no reason why thee should come in before me."

"Thou'st nought to do but to go out; I'll allow none of this so long as I am master of the house and eldest brother to thee." So saying Nicodemus took him by the arm and pushed him out, and remained himself alone with his sister by the sick girl.

Wally did not recover consciousness, she lay in a fever; her throat was swelled, her limbs stiff and aching. The brother and sister soon saw that the stranger must have suffered terribly from cold and over-fatigue, and they tended her to the best of their powers. Leander meanwhile wandered idly and restlessly through the house, and as often as one of them came out of the sick room he was in the way to enquire how things were going on. He was full of grief and vexation; he also would so willingly have tended the beautiful girl. Towards evening it ceased snowing, and he took his rifle and went out. But he had scarcely been away a minute when he came back again and called Nicodemus from the sick room. "Look here," he said, much excited, "there is a vulture on the roof, a splendid golden vulture, and he looks at me quite quietly and confidingly, as though he belonged there."

"Ah!" said Nicodemus, "that is singular."

"Only come and see," said Leander, and drew his brother out, in front of the house. "There—there he sits and never moves. A state prize, and I can't shoot him! The devil take it all!"

"Why can't thou shoot him?" asked Nicodemus.

"How can I fire now, with the sick girl lying indoors?" said Leander, stamping his foot.

"Drive him away," advised Nicodemus, "and then thou can follow him and shoot him further off where she cannot hear."

"Tsch, tsch," said Leander, throwing up balls of snow to scare off the bird. The vulture ruffled his feathers, screamed, and at last rose. But he did not fly away, he floated for a minute high in the air, and then quietly let himself down on to the roof again.

"That is strange, he won't go away; it's just as if he were tame."

Once, twice more they tried to drive it off— always with the same result.

"He's bewitched," said Leander, making the sign of the cross; but it did not seem to trouble the bird—so it was certain the devil could have nothing to do with it!

"It seems to me that he's been shot already, and cannot fly," said Nicodemus, "any way let him be in peace till he comes down of himself, if thou doesn't wish to frighten the girl with the crack of the rifle."

"He's half down already; I believe I might take him with my hand," said Leander. He fetched a ladder, laid it against the wall and cautiously ascended. The bird quietly let him approach; he drew his handkerchief from his pocket, and would have thrown it over the vulture's head, but the bird struck and pecked at him so violently, that he was obliged to beat a hasty retreat.

Nicodemus laughed. "There, he's shown thee how to catch a vulture with the hand. I could have told thee as much as that."

"I never saw such a bird in my life," said Leander grumbling, and shaking his head, "Wait a bit," he added, threatening his foe above, "only wait till I find thee somewhere else."

"Thou can hunt him to-morrow if he's not perished in the night. If he can fly, he'll go farther away, and hardly come so far as this again."

It was getting dark now, and Marianne came out to say she must go home and cook her husband's supper. The brothers went in, and Nicodemus also went to prepare supper, by fetching bread and cheese from the store room. While he was gone, Leander softly opened the door that led from the living room into the bedroom and peeped through the crack at Wally. She lay still now, and slept soundly. It was so long since she had lain in any bed, that it could be seen even in her sleep how comfortable she found it; she lay reclining so softly, so easily amongst the pillows. "God help thee, thou poor soul, God help thee!" whispered Leander to her through the opening, then hastily closed the door again, for he heard Nicodemus coming. He was sitting quite innocently on the bench by the stove when his brother came in with the food.

"To-night," said Nicodemus, "we shall do well enough; as Benedict is not here, I can sleep upstairs in his bed, but to-morrow night, when he's back again, we three must divide the two beds between us."

"Oh, I need no bed," said Leander hastily. "For the sake of her in there, I'd as soon sleep on the bench here, or in the hay-loft; it is all one to me. If any of us is to be put out for her, it shall be me, and no one else."

"Well, if it pleases thee, thou can have it so. But in the hay-loft, not on the bench; that is too near the sick-room—dost understand?"

"Ay, ay, I understand well enough," muttered Leander, and bit into his cheese as if it were a sour apple.

The bedroom of the two younger brothers was exactly opposite that of Nicodemus, who took the bed of the absent Benedict. Two or three times in the night he got up, and went to listen at Wally's door; she talked and wandered a good deal, and once Nicodemus could clearly understand that she was speaking of a vulture. "Ah," thought he, "she too will have seen the vulture when she came up, and the fright comes back to her in her dreams."

Early in the morning, before breakfast even, the restless Leander was up and out; he did not come home till nearly mid-day.

"Well, how is she getting on?" he asked as he came in.

"Just the same; she doesn't come to herself at all, and she's always in dread of people who, she thinks, want to take her away."

Leander scratched his head behind his ear. "Then I can't shoot yet. Only think now—there's the vulture outside still sitting on the roof."

"Never!"

"Ay, when I went out this morning, I couldn't see him anywhere; then I thought, he's flown away, and I went after him for nearly three hours. Then when I get home, there he is, sitting quietly on the roof again."

"Well," said Nicodemus, "that's a thing that might make one really uneasy, if one happened to be superstitious."

"Ay, indeed. One might almost think of the phantom maidens of Murzoll, and that they meant to play me a rogue's trick."

"God be praised!" said a rough deep voice, and Benedict the second brother, who had been away on a journey, now walked in.

"Ay, God be praised thou'rt back again," cried his brothers together. "What's the news? What's thou been doing?"

"Oh, nothing much; they've only sent me from Herod to Pilate again down in the Court-house, and crammed me with half-promises. I only know that all Oetzthal, man and beast of all three genders, may break neck and limb over the road here before we get the path." The speaker threw off his knapsack discontentedly and seated himself on the bench by the stove. "Is there anything to eat?" he said.

"Directly," said Nicodemus, who did the cooking himself, and he fetched in the soup.

He also brought a bowl of milk, and took it in to the sick girl; Leander's eye followed him enviously. Benedict was hungry and fell to on the soup without observing what his brother had done: Nicodemus soon returned, and silently, like all peasants, who seem to fear when performing the solemn act of eating that they will get out of time if they speak, the three spooned up the soup in a measured rhythmical movement, so that neither of them should get more nor less than his share.

When they had eaten, the weary Benedict lighted his pipe and stretched himself comfortably on the bench.

"What's the news in the world? Tell us all about it," said Leander, who knew his brother's habit of silence. Benedict had stuck his pipe aslant in his mouth and yawned. "I know of nought," he said. After a time, however, he went on: "Rich Stromminger of Sonnenplatte, his daughter, the Vulture-maiden, you know—she set her father's place on fire, and is running now about the country begging."

"Ah, when did that happen?" asked the brothers astonished.

"She must be a real bad girl that," continued Benedict. "Her father had sent her up to the Hochjoch before this, because she wouldn't do his bidding, and when she comes down, the first thing is that she half kills Gellner, and sets her father's house on fire."

"Jesu Maria!"

"After that she naturally ran away, and is now

wandering about the neighbourhood. Yesterday she was in Vent, and trying to get a place, but who would have such a girl in the house? To add to it all, she drags the big vulture about with her that she took from the nest, and expects folk to take that in too. Naturally every one refuses."

Nicodemus looked at Leander, and Leander grew crimson.

"Well!—" said Nicodemus, "now I know who's lying in there!—The vulture that won't leave the roof—and all night she was raving about a vulture —that's not so bad—we've the Vulture-maiden in the house!"

Benedict sprang up. "What!" he cried.

"Don't cry out so loud," said Leander, "dost want the poor sick girl to hear it all?"

Then Nicodemus related how Leander had found her half dead in the snow, and how they could not do otherwise than keep her in the house, at least till she was able to walk. But Benedict was a rough man, and thought the illness was only a pretence —that his brothers had been too soft and should have sent her away. He would soon have got the better of her. "For incendiaries he had no sanctuary," he cried, and his piercing eyes glanced wrathfully under his bushy brows.

"If thou'd seen the maid, thou'd have taken her

in too," said Leander, "It'd have been less than human to turn the poor thing out in the wind and weather."

"Indeed? And in that way we should get at last every robber and murderer in the neighbourhood in asylum here, till it is said that Rofen is a hiding-place for all the rabble — that'd be a fine thing for the justices to get hold of. If you two can be taken in by a cunning chit, I at least must maintain order and decency in Rofen!"

He approached the door. Nicodemus stood before it and said quietly, but firmly, "Benedict, I am the eldest, and I'm master in Rofen as much as thou, and I know as well as thou what is our duty as Rofeners. I give thee my word I will keep the girl no longer in the house than I must for human and Christian duty; but now she is sick, and I will not suffer thee to ill-use her. So long as I live at Rofen I'll have no injustice done under my roof."

Then Leander broke in. "Look here," he said confidently and with flashing eyes; "only let him go in — when he sees her, he'll never send her away."

"I believe thou'rt right, thou simpleton," said Nicodemus smiling, and he softly opened the door.

Benedict hastily and noisily entered; this time Leander ventured to slip in also, and Nicodemus had nothing to say against it; he might help to watch over the harsh Benedict and keep him

from being too rough. Marianne was sitting by the
bed making new stockings for the sick girl, for she
had become so ragged that she would have had none
to wear when she could get up again. At Benedict's
noisy entrance she made a sign that he should be
quiet; but scarcely had he perceived the sick girl,
when of himself he hushed his footsteps, and went
slowly up to the bed. Wallburga was fast asleep.
She lay on her back, and had thrown one beautiful
rounded arm over her head; her abundant dark-
brown hair fell loosely over the snow-white neck
that no sunshine could tan through her thick
peasant's bodice, and which her loose linen chemise
now left partly uncovered; her mouth was half-
open as though smiling, and two rows of pearly
teeth shone between the arched lips; on the sleeping brow lay an unspoken expression of nobility
and purity that no words can describe. Benedict
had grown quite still. He gazed long at the
touching and yet innocent picture as if astonished,
and his brown face began gradually to redden—like
Leander's, which seemed dyed in a crimson glow.
Then he ground his teeth together and turned
round. "Aye, she is certainly ill," he said in a
voice which implied, "There is nothing to be done,"
and he went out of the room on tiptoe.

CHAPTER IX.

In the Wilderness.

ONCE again spring-breezes blew across the land. The melting snows flowed down in rushing mountain-torrents; timidly, half-suspiciously the first Alpine plants peeped out, as though to ask the sunshine if it were indeed in earnest, and they might venture forth a little further. Here and there isolated patches of snow still lay like forgotten linen sheets. In the evergreen pine and fir-woods, the birds lifted their wings, held twittering consultations, and attuned their little throats to the universal song of rejoicing.

From the Ferner mountains avalanches came thundering down into the valleys, and beneath the terrible, moving masses, walls and rafters, trees and bushes, crashed together. There was a thronging and wrestling, a thundering and rustling—there were threats and allurements, fears and hopes, in the heights and in the valleys, and man also, ever-venturesome, ever-inquisitive man, arose from his long winter's rest, stretched forth his feelers, and began to grope

9*

about the mountains with his alpenstock for some foothold in the loose and shifting snow.

Only Rofen yet lay in the shadow of its narrow, heaven-high walls, hidden like a late sleeper beneath its white coverlet. Before the door of the Rofen farm stood Leander, feeding Hansl with a big mouse that he had caught for him. Hansl had been Leander's pet from the hour when it came out that he belonged to Wally, and the bird was well cared for among the Rofeners.

Benedict came towards the house with his mountain pole. He had been reconnoitring the path to Murzoll, and had more than once hovered between life and death. His glance was unsteady, his whole appearance agitated and gloomy.

"Well?" asked Leander in anxious suspense.

"The road is passable at need. If I guide her, she can risk it."

"Nay, Benedict, don't thee do that, don't let her go up there—I pray thee, don't."

"What she will—she will," said Benedict gloomily.

"Tell her the mountain's not safe, then she'll remain of herself."

"Where's the good of lying? She'll not change her mind however long she stays here, and thou hast nothing to hope, I've told thee that often enough. An unfledged stripling like thee is not for a maid like Wally! Now keep thyself quiet." He went into the house, and the tears sprang into Leander's eyes with anger and pain.

Wally came with the hayfork out of the stable towards Benedict.

"Wally," he said, "if it must be so, I'll lead thee up there, I've found out the way; but it is still dangerous."

"Thank thee kindly, Benedict," said Wally, "to-morrow, then, we will go." She hung up the hay-fork, and went into the kitchen. Benedict stamped with his foot, and set his alpenstock in the corner. For a while he stood reflecting, then he could keep quiet no longer—he followed her.

Wally had tucked up her gown and was preparing to wash the kitchen.

"Wally, leave all that, I want to talk with thee."

"I cannot, Benedict, I must scour the kitchen. If I go away to-morrow, I must have the whole house clean. I'll leave no dirt or disorder behind me."

"Thou's always worked more by us than thou hast eaten or drunken. Let be now, the house is clean enough, and if thou goes away—all is one." He chewed at a piece of wood, then spit out the bitten splinter. Wally saw the terrible state of excitement he was in, and left off her work that she might listen to him.

"Wally," he said, "consider once more whether thou'll not have one of us. See now, thou'st no need to be so proud. There's such a cry against thee, that it's through great love only, that one can take thee at all."

Wally nodded her head in perfect agreement.

"Now see, we Rofeners, we are people who may knock at every door, and there's not a girl but would be glad to get one of us. Thou hast the choice between two of us brothers, and refusest such a piece of luck. See, Wally, thou may some day repent of it."

"Benedict, thou means well, and I care for thee and Leander as one can care for only one person, but not enough to marry you. And I'll marry no one that I can't love as a husband, and that thou may know that I mean it, I once saw one that I can never forget, and till I do forget him, I'll take no other."

Benedict grew pale.

"See, I tell thee that thou may be at peace, and no longer torment thyself with the thought of me. Only believe, Benedict, I know well what thou hast done, thou and all of you for me. You saved me from death, you protected me when my father'd have taken me away by force, and it was really fine how thou defended me and thy rights. I'd be a happy girl if I could love thee and forget that other. I'm right thankful to thee, and if it could help thee, I'd give thee my life—but tell thyself, what would thee do with a wife who loves some one else? That were truly a bad return to a man like thee."

"Yes," said Benedict hoarsely, and wiped his forehead.

"And thou sees now, that I must go away, that things can't go on as they are?"

"Yes," he said again, and left the kitchen.

Wally looked after him as, full of emotion, he strode away, the brave and proud man who had offered her all, all that—as he himself had said in his uncouth fashion—would have made the happiness of any other girl. And she herself could not understand how it was that she could not care more for this man, who had done so much for her, than for the stranger who had never once given her a thought. And yet so it was! There was not one who could be compared with Joseph for power and excellence; she saw him always before her as when he had flung the bloody bear's skin from his shoulder and related how he had wrestled with the monster, whilst all stood around and admired him, the mighty, the beautiful, the only one! And then how he had conquered her father, the strong man who had always appeared to her hitherto so unconquerable and terrible! And with what goodness and kindness he had spoken to him afterwards, in spite of her father's hostility! No, there was not one that could rise up and stand comparison with Joseph.

She went back to her work. "If only Joseph knew all that I am giving up for his sake," she thought as she looked out, and saw how in front of the window Benedict with a red face was talking to Leander, and how Leander wept.

Old Stromminger had at first stormed against and cursed his unruly child, and not even the good pastor of Heiligkreuz had succeeded in pacifying him. When it was at length rumoured that Wally kept herself hidden at Rofen, he sent people to fetch her away. But on their own ground and territory it was easy for no one to move the "Klötze of Rofen," and they defended like knights the sacred rights and freedom of the Rofeners. When Wally however perceived that a passion for her had taken possession of the brothers, then she made a confidant of the quiet and prudent Nicodemus, and he understood what was needful to be done. He went to Stromminger, and his wise eloquence was so far successful that the old man at last gave up the idea of imprisoning Wally, and contented himself with banishing her for ever from his sight. In the summer she should tend the flocks again upon Murzoll, "because that is the only way in which one can make any use of her." In the winter she might seek service wherever she liked— only she was not to venture to come back to her home.

When Nicodemus returned with this answer, Wally insisted upon going that moment to await the flocks upon the Ferner, and only Nicodemus' firm decision prevailed upon her to wait at least till Benedict should have examined whether the mountain road were passable.

So the hour came when Wally must once more fly before the winds of spring on to the mountains, into the desert. It was hard to part with the brothers, and with good Marianne. They had become dear to her, these worthy people, who had come so readily to her help.

Benedict went up the mountain with her; he would not let himself be deprived of that. "Thou'st been entrusted to us, we will at least hand thee back again with a whole skin. Whatever may happen to thee then, we can, alas! do nought to hinder."

It was a fearful road up which they had to make their way in the midst of the wild confusion wrought by the spring, and Benedict, acknowledged far and

wide to be the best and surest of guides, said himself he had never seen so bad a mountain-path.
They spoke little, for they were engaged in a con-
stant, breathless struggle for life, and could look
neither to the right nor to the left. It was hard
work. At length, after fighting half the day with
snow and ice and crevasses, they found themselves
on the summit. The old hut still stood there, somewhat more ruinous than before, and a heavy weight
of snow lay on the roof and all around it.

"There thou means to house thyself—there!
Sooner than become an honoured wife and lead
with us down yonder a respected and home-sheltered
life as a peasant of Rofen?"

"I can do no other, Benedict," said Wally gently,
and looked with sad eyes at the snow-covered inhospitable hut. "I believe the mountain spirits have
thrown a spell upon me, so that I must needs come
back to them, and never more feel myself at home
in the valleys."

"One might almost believe it! There's something strange about thee. Thou's quite different
from other maids, so that one loves thee in quite
a different way—much, much more dearly, and yet
as if thou didn't belong to us, as if an evil spirit
drove thee round."

He threw down the bundle of provisions that he

had brought up with him for Wally, and began re-moving the snow from the door of the hut that she might be able to get into it.

"Benedict," said Wally softly, as though she could be overheard, "dost thou believe in the phantom maidens?"

Benedict looked down meditatively and shrugged his shoulders. "What can one say? I've never seen any myself—but there are people who'd hold to it to their last breath."

"I'd never believed in them—but when I came up here last year, I had a dream so lifelike, I could almost believe it was no dream, and since then, whatever happens to me, I can't help thinking of the phantom-maidens."

"What sort of a dream?"

"Thou must know that him whom I love is a chamois-hunter, and it was because of him my father sent me up last year, and the first hour I was here I dreamt that the phantom-maidens and Murzoll threatened me that if I wouldn't leave off thinking of the lad, they'd fling me down into the abyss!" And she related her whole dream in detail to Benedict. He shook his head, and became quite melancholy. "Wally, in thy place, I should be afraid."

She threw her head back. "Ah well. Thou goes

on shooting the chamois, in spite of the phantom-maidens. One has only got not to be afraid. I've sprung over many a chasm since then, and I've felt well enough that there was somewhat that wished to pull me down, but I held myself firm, and kept the upper hand."

She raised her strong brown arm defiantly. "So long as I've got two arms, I've no need to fear whatever it may be."

This did not please Benedict. In his solitary wanderings over the terrible Similaun and the wild glacier peaks, he had acquired a taste for subtle meditations and reflected more deeply on many things than other people. "Take care, Wally! He who sets himself too high thrusts his head up easily enough, but that's what those up yonder won't endure, and they thrust him down again."

She was silent.

"It's too early for thee to be up here—" he began again, "no one could stand it."

"Oh, it was worse still when I was up here last autumn," said Wally, as she went into the hut.

"Who won't be advised, can't be helped. But if *he* doesn't some time recompense thee for all thou'rt going through for him, he deserves to be dragged round by the collar."

"If he knew of it, for sure he'd recompense me," said Wally reddening and looking down.

"He doesn't know of it?" asked Benedict astonished.

"No, he scarcely knows me."

"Now may God forgive thee that thou should so set thy heart on a strange man, and them, them who love thee, and have cherished thee and tended thee, them thou pushes from thee. That is no love —that is mere obstinacy."

Wally was silent, and Benedict also said no more. He did now as old Klettenmaier had done the year before. He set the hut in order as well as he could for Wally, and brought her a store of wood. Then he held out his hand to her in farewell. "May God guard thee up here! And if I might say one more word to thee, it would be this: Watch over thyself, and pray that no evil powers may get the better of thee!"

Wally's heart contracted as his eyes full of deep sadness rested on her. It seemed to her as though in truth she felt the evil powers hovering round her, and almost unconsciously she held the hand of her protector who had watched over her so faithfully, and accompanied him part of the way back, as though she feared to remain alone.

"Now then—here the path becomes bad; I thank

thee for coming so far," said Benedict, and parted from her.

"Farewell, and a safe journey home," cried Wally after him.

He looked round no more. She turned back to the hut, and was once more alone with her vulture and her mountain spirits. But the spirits seemed appeased. Murzoll smiled kindly in the glow of the spring sunshine upon the returned child, and Wally no longer felt herself a stranger in the midst of her mighty and sublime surroundings. Each fold on Murzoll's brow was familiar to her now; she knew his smile and his frown, and it no longer frightened her when sullen clouds beset his brow, or when he rolled down avalanches into the abyss. She felt herself secure on his harsh breast, and the breath of his storms blew away from her heart the weight that she had brought up with her again from the valley. For a healing power lies in the storm; it cools the blood, it bears the soul on its rushing wings far away over the stones and thorns amongst which it would flutter, painfully entangled. As when a child has hurt itself and cries, we breathe on the place, saying, "It will soon be well," and the child smiles back to us again, so Father Murzoll blew away from the heart of his returned child the dull pain that oppressed it, and she looked with shining eyes and an uplifted heart out into the wide world—and hoped and waited.

So weeks and months passed by. The July sun shone with such power that the mountain was already completely "ausgeapert"; that is to say, the lighter winter snow was all melted away to the limits of the eternal snows where Wally dwelt. Now and then one of the Rofener brothers came up to enquire whether she had not yet changed her mind. But they came but seldom, and interrupted Wally's solitude by a few short half-hours only.

One day the sun's rays "pricked" with such sharp, unusual heat, that Wally felt as though she were passing between glowing needles. When the sun "pricks," it draws the clouds together, and soon, somewhere about midday, it had gathered about itself a thick tent of clouds behind which it disappeared, and a leaden twilight was spread heavily over the earth. A strange disquietude seized the little flock; now and then a quivering brightness shuddered through the grey cloud-chaos, as a sleeper's eyelashes quiver in dreams, and gigantic black mourning clouds waved about Murzoll's head. Now and again they were rent asunder, affording faint glimpses into the clear distance, but instantly across these thin places new veils were woven till all was closed, and no empty space, as it seemed, left between earth and Heaven.

Wally well knew what all this foreboded; she had already experienced plenty of bad weather up here on the mountains, and she drove the flock together under a projecting rock, where she had herself arranged a fold in case of need. But a young goat had wandered out of sight, and she was obliged to go and seek it. No storm had ever yet come on with such rapidity. Already hollow mutterings could be heard amongst the mountains, whilst the gusts of wind swept roaring onwards, flinging down isolated hailstones. Now it was a question of minutes only, and the kid was nowhere to be seen. Wally extinguished her hearth fire and stepped out into the conflict of the elements, like an heroic queen amongst the hosts of her rebellious subjects. And queen-like indeed she looked, without knowing or caring anything about it. She had set a little copper milk-can upside down upon her head as a helmet to protect her from the hailstones, and a thick horse-cloth hung down like a mantle from her shoulders. Thus equipped, and a shepherd's staff with its iron hook in her hand in the place of a lance, she threw herself out into the storm, and fought her way through it till she reached a point of rock from whence she could look out after the lost animal.

But it was impossible through the mists to distinguish anything. Wally ascended higher and higher, till she had reached the path that leads over the Hochjoch into the Schnalser valley; and there, deep below in the ravine, the kid was clinging to the side of the steep precipice, trembling with fear and crouching beneath the blows of the heavy hailstones. The helpless animal moved her to pity—she must have compassion on it. The hail rattled down thicker and thicker around her, the wind and rain struck her like whips across the face, there was a heaving and swelling on every side like the thundering waves of an approaching deluge, but she paid no heed to it; the mute supplications of the distressed animal rose above the raging of the storm, and without a moment's hesitation she let herself down into the misty depths. With infinite trouble she got far enough down the slippery path to lay hold of the animal with her crook and draw it towards her, then throwing it over her shoulder, she climbed upwards again with hands and feet. Then, all at once, a stream of fire seemed to shoot from the zenith down into the gulf, a shivered fir-tree crashed beneath her in the depths, and in one universal roar of heaven and earth together there came a crackling from above, a rushing, a thundering of hurling streams and masses below, till to the solitary pilgrim clinging to the quaking rock it seemed as though the whole world were whirling round her in wild dissolution. Half-stunned, she swung herself up at last on to the firm edge of the pathway, then stood a moment to recover breath and wipe the moisture from her eyes, for she could hardly see, and the kid too struggled on her shoulder, so that she was obliged to bind it before carrying it any further. Meanwhile, thunder-clap after thunder-clap crashed above her, beneath her, and as though heaven had been a leaking cask filled with fire, the lightning struck downwards in fiery streams. Hark!—what was that?—a human voice! A cry for help sounded clearly above the rushing and roaring. Wally who had not trembled at the fury of the thunder and the hurricane, trembled now. A human voice—now!—up here with her in this fearful tumult of nature, in this chaos! It terrified her more than the raging of the elements. She listened with suspended breath to hear whence the voice came, and whether she had not deceived herself. Again she heard the cry, and close behind her. "Hi, thou yonder—help me, then!" And out of the mists and rain emerged a figure that seemed to drag along a second form. Wally stood as though suddenly stiffened—what face was that? The burning eyes, the black moustache, the finely aquiline nose, she looked and looked and could not stir a limb for the sweet terror that had come upon her—it was indeed St. George, it was Joseph the bear-hunter.

He himself was scarcely less startled than Wally when she turned round, but from another cause. "Jesu Maria—it's a girl," he said almost timidly, and looked at Wally with astonishment. Seeing her from behind, he had thought from her height that she was a shepherd—now he saw a maiden before him. And as she stood there, her long mantle falling around her in stiff folds, her head protected by its warlike helmet against the hail, her dark hair, loosened and dripping, hanging about her face, the crook in her hand and the kid on her broad shoulders, her great eyes flaming and fastened upon him, he had a weird feeling for a moment, as though something supernatural stood before him. In his whole life before he had never seen so powerful a woman, and he had to pause for a minute before he could clearly make her out.

"Ah," he said, "thou'rt only old Stromminger's Vulture-Wally?"

"Yes, that am I," answered the girl breathlessly.

"So—well, precisely then with thee I have nothing to do."

"Why not?" asked Wally, turning pale, and a

flash of lightning quivered just over her, so that her copper helmet flashed red in the glare.

Joseph was obliged to pause, so crashing was the thunder-clap that followed, and with new fury a shower of hail came rattling down. Joseph looked at the girl in perplexity as she stood there immovable, whilst lumps of ice struck against the slight metal can on her head. Then he bent down over the lifeless form that he was carrying.

"See here, ever since that affair in Sölden I've been in disgrace with thy father, and people say that thou also art not one to have dealings with. But this poor maid can go no further; a flash of lightning struck close by her and threw her down, and she's quite out of her senses. Go, lead us to thy hut, that the girl may rest till the storm is over —then we'll leave again at once; and for certain, such a thing shall never happen again."

Wally looked strangely at him during this speech —half in defiance, half in pain. Her lips trembled as though she would have made some vehement answer, but she controlled herself, and after a short and silent struggle, "Come," she said, and strode onwards before him. Presently she paused and asked, "Who is the maid?"

"She's a poor girl out of Vintschgau on her way to the Lamb in Zwieselstein. My mother is dead, and I've had to go over to Vintschgau, where her home was, to look after the inheritance, and as our roads lay together, I've brought the girl across the mountains with me," answered Joseph evasively.

"Thy mother is dead? Oh, thou poor Joseph—" cried Wally full of sympathy.

"Yes—it was a hard blow," said Joseph in deep sadness, "the good little mother."

Wally saw that it pained him to speak of her, and was silent. They said no more till they reached the hut.

"Here's a horrible hole," said Joseph stooping and yet knocking his head as he entered. "It's not for nothing that a man sends his child off to live in a dog-kennel like this. Well, certainly thou'st done enough to deserve it."

"Ah!—thou's sure of that?" said Wally, breaking out bitterly now as she untied the kid and set it down in a corner. Then she shook up her bed and helped Joseph to lay the stranger on it. Her hands trembled as she did so.

"Well," said Joseph indifferently, "everyone knows how wild thou's been with thy father, and how thou nearly killed Vincenz Gellner dead, and set fire to thy father's barn in a rage. It seems to me, that with such a beginning thou may go still further."

"Dost know *why* I struck Vincenz, and fired the barn?" asked Wally with a trembling voice, "Dost know *why* I am up here in this dog-kennel as thou calls it? Dost know?" And with her two hands she broke a strong branch in pieces across her knee, so that the wood cracked and splintered, and Joseph involuntarily admired her strength.

"No," he said, "how should I know?"

"Well then, if thou doesn't know, thou needn't speak of it," she said low and angrily as she made up the fire that she might warm some milk for the sick girl.

"Tell me, then, if thou thinks I'm doing thee a wrong."

Wally broke out again suddenly into the shrill, bitter laugh peculiar to her when her heart was secretly bleeding. "Thee I'm to tell—thee?" she cried, "Yes, truly; thou'rt a fitting person for me to tell!" And she rinsed out a kettle with feverish haste, poured the milk into it, and hung it up over the crackling fire.

Joseph did not discover the pain that lay hidden in this scorn—he only felt the scorn, and turned away from her offended: "With thee there's nothing to be said; people are right enough there," he answered, and thenceforward occupied himself only with the sick girl.

Wally also was silent, and only now and then as she moved about her work cast a stolen glance to where Joseph, with the red light of the fire upon him, sat on a stool not far from the bed. His eyes glowed like two coals in the reflection of the flames, which shining now brightly, now faintly, lighted up the strong and handsome face of the hunter with strange changes, so that it appeared sometimes friendly, sometimes full of gloom.

All at once Wally remembered her dream on the first night of her arrival on the Hochjoch. "If the phantom-maidens could see him now, they would melt away before him like snow before the fire." Something of this she thought, and it seemed to her as if only with tears of blood—as it is said of a heart that it bleeds—could she tear her glance away from him. Two scalding drops did in truth fall from her eyes, and though they were not drops of blood, they gave her no less pain.

The stranger now recovered consciousness. "What has happened?" she asked in astonishment.

"Thou must keep thyself quiet, Afra," said Joseph, "the lightning nearly struck thee dead, and so Wally Stromminger has brought us to her hut."

"Jesu Maria, are we with the Vulture-Wally?" said the girl terrified.

"Keep thyself still," said Joseph, comforting her,

"as soon as thou's recovered, we'll go on our way again."

"So over in Vintschgau even thou's heard talk of me? There, take something to drink against the fright," said Wally quietly and with a touch of good-humoured sarcasm, as she reached her the warm milk mixed with some brandy. Joseph had stood up to allow Wally to come to the bed with the drink. Afra tried to sit up but she could not manage it, and Wally coming quickly to her aid raised her and held her in her arms like a child, whilst she gave her the milk with the other hand. Afra took a thirsty draught out of the wooden bowl, but she was so weak that her head sank upon Wally's shoulder when she had done drinking, and Wally, beckoning to Joseph to take the bowl from her hand, remained sitting patiently so as not to disturb the sick girl.

Joseph looked at her meditatively, as she sat there on the edge of the bed with the girl in her arms. "Thou'rt a handsome maid," he said honestly, "it's a pity only thou should be so bad."

A slight colour passed over Wally's face at these words.

"How thy heart beats all at once!" said Afra. "I can feel it on thy shoulder." And a little stronger now, she raised her head and gazed at the beautiful tanned face, and the large eyes. Wally also now studied the girl more attentively. She saw that she had charming features, blue eyes full of expression, fair hair that looked like floss silk, and a strange, uneasy feeling of aversion stole over her. She looked at Joseph, stood up, and began to bustle round again.

"Is that really the Vulture-Wally?" asked Afra of her guide, as though she could not understand how the decried Vulture-maiden could be so kind.

"One wouldn't suppose it, but she says herself that it's she," answered Joseph half-aloud.

"And I'll soon prove to thee that I am," cried Wally proudly, and opening the door, she cried "Hansl—Hansl, where art thou?" A shrill scream answered her, and forthwith Hansl came rushing down from the roof, and in at the door.

"Heavens, what is that?" screamed Afra, crossing herself; but Joseph placed himself before her, as a protector.

"That is the vulture that I took as a child out of its nest—away yonder on the Burgsteinwand. It is from him I got my name—the Vulture-maiden!" and her eyes rested proudly on the bird, as a soldier's eyes rest on the conquered colours. "See, I've tamed him so that I can let him fly where he likes now—he never flies away from me." She set him on her shoulder and unfolded his wings, so that Joseph might see they were not cut.

"That fellow's a state-prize," said Joseph, his eyes resting with both longing and hostility on the splendid booty which no hunter will yield to another, least of all to a girl! There must have been something in the look that irritated the vulture, for he uttered a peculiar whistle, bristled up his feathers, and bent his neck forward towards Joseph. Wally felt the unwonted agitation on her shoulder and tried to quiet the bird with caresses. "Nay, Hansl, what's come to thee? Thou wert never so before."

"Aha!—thou knows the hunter, my fine fellow," said Joseph with a challenging laugh and snatching violently at the vulture as though to tear him from Wally's shoulder. Suddenly the irritated bird put forth all its might, spread out its wings, rose to the ceiling, and thence swooped with its whole strength down upon the enemy below. A shriek of terror rang from Wally's lips, Afra saved herself in a corner, the narrow hut was almost filled with the rushing monster who no longer heard his mistress's voice, but dashed again and again at Joseph with his terrible beak striving to strike his talons into the man's side. It was one wild confusion of fighting fists and wings, in which feathers flew about, and the walls grew red where Joseph's bleeding hands touched them. "My knife, if I could only get at my knife," he cried.

Wally tore the door open. "Out, Joseph, out into the open air; in this narrow hole thou can do nothing with him."

But Joseph the bear-slayer had no idea of running away from a vulture. "The devil take me if I stir from the spot," he said with a groan. For one moment longer the battle wavered. Then Joseph, his face pressed against the wall, managed with his iron fists to seize the vulture by the claws, and with giant strength forced down the struggling animal as in a trap whilst it hacked at his hands and arms with its beak. "Now my knife, draw out my knife—I have no hand free," he cried to Wally.

But Wally used the moment otherwise; she sprang by, and threw a thick cloth over the vulture's head. It was easy for her now to tie its feet together with a cord, so as to render it helpless, and Joseph flung it on the ground. Trembling and without strength the proud animal exhausted itself in struggles in the cloth on the floor, and Joseph taking up his gun, began to load it.

"What art thou doing there?" asked Wally astonished.

"Loading my gun," he said, setting his teeth with the pain of his torn hands. When it was loaded, he took the captive bird up from the floor, and flung it out of the hut into the open air. Then placing himself at a little distance, he took aim, and said low and imperiously to Wally, "Now let him loose."

" *What* am I to do?" said Wally, who could not believe she had heard aright.

"Let him fly!"

"What for?"

"That I may shoot him. Doesn't thee know that no true hunter shoots his game excepting on the spring or on the wing?"

"For God's sake," cried Wally, "thou wouldn't shoot me my Hansl?"

Joseph, in his turn, looked at her wonderingly. "Thou'd have me let the rabid brute live, perhaps?" he said.

"Joseph," said Wally, stepping resolutely up to him, "leave me my Hansl untouched. I fought with the old one for the bird at the risk of my life, I've brought him up from the nest, no one loves me as he does—he's my only one, all that I have in the world—thou shall do nothing to my Hansl."

"Indeed," said Joseph sharply and bitterly, "the

devil nearly tore out my eyes, and I shall do nothing to him?"

"He didn't know thee. How can a bird help it that he has no more sense? Thou'll never revenge thyself on a beast without understanding?"

Joseph stamped his foot. "Unbind him that he may fly," he said, "or I'll shoot him in a heap, as he is." He took aim again with his rifle.

All the hot blood flew to Wally's head, and she forgot everything but her favourite. "That we will see," she cried in flaming anger, "whether thou'll dare to lay hands on my property. Put down the gun. The bird is mine! Dost hear? *Mine.* And none shall hurt or harm him when I am by, come what will. Away with the gun, or thou shall learn to know who *I* am!" And she struck the gun out of his hand with a swift blow, so that the charge went off, rattling against the wall of rock.

There was something in her demeanour that subdued the strong young fellow, the mighty bear-hunter, for he picked up his gun with apparent composure, saying with bitter scorn, "Please thyself for all I care; I'll not touch thy hook-beaked sweetheart; he's like enough the only one thou'll ever have in thy life! Thou—thou's nothing but the Vulture-Wally."

And without deigning even to look at her again

he tore his pocket-handkerchief into strips, and tried to bind up his torn hands with it. Wally sprung forward and would have helped him; now for the first time she saw how severe the wounds were, and it was as if her own heart were bleeding at the sight. "O Heavens, lad, what hands thou'st got!" she cried out. "Come, and I'll wash them and dress them for thee."

But Joseph shoved her aside. "Let be—Afra can do it," he said.

He went into the hut. An anguish as of death came over Wally; she suddenly understood that she had made Joseph her enemy, perhaps for ever, and she felt as if she must die at the thought. As though suddenly crushed, she followed him in, and her eye watched the stranger as she bound up Joseph's hands, with jealous hatred.

"Joseph," said she in a stifled voice, "thee mustn't think that I don't care for thy wounds, because I wouldn't let thee shoot my Hansl. If it could have made thy hands whole, thou might have shot Hansl first, and me after him; but it would have done thee no good."

"It's no matter, there's no need to excuse thyself," said Joseph, turning away. "Afra," he continued to the girl, "can thou go on now?"

"Yes," she said.

"Make thyself ready then, we'll go."

Wally turned pale. "Joseph, thou must rest thyself a little longer. I've given thee nothing yet to eat; I will cook thee something at once, or would thou sooner have a draught of milk?"

"I thank thee kindly; but we must go so as to be home before nightfall. It no longer rains, and Afra can walk again now." And with these words he helped the girl to get ready, slung his gun over his shoulder, and took his alpenstock in his hand.

Wally picked up one of the feathers which had fallen from Hansl in the struggle, and stuck it in Joseph's hat. "Thou must wear the feather, Joseph. Thou ought to wear it, for thou conquered the vulture, and he'd have been thy booty if thou'd not given him to me."

But Joseph took the feather out of his hat. "Thou may mean well," he said, "but the feather I'll not wear. I'm not accustomed to share my booty with girls."

"Then take the vulture altogether, I'll give him to thee; only I pray thee, let him live," urged Wally breathlessly.

Joseph looked at her in wonder. "What has come to thee?" he said, "I'll take nothing from thee on which thy heart is so set; one day perhaps I may take a live bear, and if so I'll bring it up to thee that the party may be complete. But till then, thou'll see no more of me; I might happen to shoot the bird yet if I came across him anywhere, so I'd better keep away from his haunts! God be with thee, and thanks for the shelter thou's given us." So saying he walked proudly and quietly out of the hut.

Afra stooped down and picked up the feather that Joseph had thrown away. "Give me the feather," she said; "I'll lay it in my prayer-book, and so often as I see it I will say a Pater Noster for thee."·

"As thou will," said Wally gloomily; she had scarcely heard what Afra had said. Her bosom heaved and throbbed, and in her ears there was a rushing noise as though the tempest was still raging round her. She followed the departing guests out of the hut. The storm had passed away; the veil of black clouds hung raggedly down, and through the rents sparkled the wet, far-gleaming distance. But for the sullen mutterings of the Thunder-god as he withdrew, and the roar of the waters as they rushed down the gullies into the depths, all around was tranquil and silent, and a white shroud of snow and hail stones had spread itself upon the mountains.

Wally stood motionless, her hands pressed upon

her bosom. "He never thinks how poor one must be to set one's heart so upon a bird," said she to herself. Then she stooped down and freed the half-numbed animal that climbed, staggering, on to her arm and looked at her with intelligence, as if to ask her forgiveness. "Aye, thou may look at me," she sobbed; "oh, Hansl, Hansl, what hast thou done for me!"

She sat down on the door-step of her little hut, and wept from the very bottom of her heart till she was weary of the sound of her own sobbing. She looked up to where a high wall of snow rose perpendicularly behind her, down to where on the right hand and on the left death had prepared his cold nest in the snowy hollows,—away into the grey distance, where long streaks of rain cloud hung down from heaven to earth, and suddenly she felt again as she had felt on the first day, that she was alone in the wilderness—and must stay there.

CHAPTER X.

The Mistress of the Sonnenplatte.

AGAIN a year had gone by, a hard year for Wally; for when her lonely summer in the wilds was ended and Stromminger had sent to fetch the flocks home, she had gone down into the Schnalser valley on the other side of the Ferner where she was quite a stranger, and there had sought service. To the Rofeners she would not return, as she must again have rejected their suit. But it was just as hard to find employment with the vulture here as it had been in the Oetz valley, and at last she gave up all thought of remuneration, only to be taken in with Hansl. Naturally her lot was a forlorn one— for on account of this folly, as they called it, she was often turned away or scornfully treated by the women; and often she had to defend herself stoutly against the rude importunities of the men, who, here as everywhere, admired the beautiful girl. Nevertheless she bore it all steadfastly, for she was too proud to lament and complain of a burden she had laid on herself of her own free will. But she grew hard under it, hard and ever harder, just as the good pastor had forewarned her. The ghosts of all the murdered joys of her young life haunted her and cried out for revenge; in the short spring time of life three lost years count for much. Other young girls weep and lament over a lost dance. Wally did not weep for all the lost dances, for all the thousand pleasures of her youth, she grieved only for her wasted love; and her spirit, on which no ray of happiness had shone, waxed sour and hard like a fruit that has matured in the shade.

Again the spring time came, and again Wally ascended the Ferner. It was a bitter spring and a stormy summer; rain, snow, and hail succeeded each other in turns, so that her clothes often did not dry the whole day through, and for weeks together she breathed the damp atmosphere of an impenetrable chaos of drizzling clouds, through which, as before the first day of Creation, no ray of light would dawn. And, in her soul, the vast outer chaos reproduced itself in little, gloom reflected gloom. The whole world as yet was but a dark and troubled dream like the cloud drifts around her—and God came not, who alone could say, "Let there be Light."

One day, however, after endless weeks of darkness, He spoke again the mighty word of creation, and a gleam of sunshine shot through the clouds and parted them, and gradually there emerged from the chaos a fair and well-ordered world, with mountains and valleys, pastures and lakes and forests; it was spread out suddenly complete before her eyes, and she felt as if she also were now first suddenly roused to life—as was once the mother of mankind—that she might rejoice in this world that God had made so beautiful, not for Himself alone, but for those beings whom He had created to take delight in it with Him.

Was it possible there should be no happiness in so fair a world? And wherefore had God set her, this hapless Eve, up here in the desert, where he for whom she had been born could never find her? "Oh! yonder, down yonder—enough of these lonely heights!" a voice cried suddenly within her, and all at once the wild yearning for life, for love, for happiness broke forth, so that she longingly stretched out her arms towards the smiling, sunny world that lay below at her feet.

"Wally, thou must come down at once. Thy father's dead." The shepherd boy stood before her.

Wally stared at him as if dreaming. Was it a vision called up by her own heart, that even now had cried out so rebelliously for happiness? She grasped the lad by the shoulder as though to assure herself that he was indeed there, and it was no trick of the imagination. He repeated the message. "The place in his foot got worse and worse, then it mortified, and he died this morning. Now thou's mistress at the farm, and Klettenmaier sends thee greeting."

Then it was true, really true! the messenger of release, of peace, of liberty stood before her in the flesh. For this it was that God had shown her the earth so fair, as though He would say to her beforehand, "See, this is now thine own, come down and take that which I have given thee."

She went silently into the hut and closed the door. Then she knelt down and thanked God, and prayed—prayed again, for the first time in many weeks, ardently, from the depth of her soul; and hot tears for the father who was now for ever gone —whom living she could not and dared not love as a child—welled up from her released and reconciled heart.

Then she went down to the home, that now at last was again a home to her, where her foot once more trod her own soil, her own hearth. Old Klettenmaier stood at the gate and joyfully waved his cap when she arrived; the servant-girl who, two years before, had been so rude to her, came weeping and submissive to give her the keys, and at the sitting-room door she was received by Vincenz.

"Wally," he began, "thou'st used me very badly, but—"

Wally interrupted him quietly but severely. "Vincenz, if I've done thee any wrong, may God punish me as it shall please Him. I cannot regret it nor make it good to thee, nor do I ask thee for forgiveness. Now thou know'st my mind, and all I pray thee is, leave me to myself."

And without vouchsafing him another glance, she went in to where the body of her father lay, and locked the door. She stood by it, tearless. She had been able to weep for the transfigured father, freed from the "tenement of clay;" but standing by that form of clay itself, which with a heavy fist had marred her and her life, which had struck her down and trodden on her—she could shed no tears, she was as if made of stone.

Quietly she said a Pater Noster, but she did not kneel to say it. As she had stood motionless, self-possessed before her living father, so now she stood before him dead; only without resentment, reconciled by death.

Then she went into the kitchen to prepare a

supper by the time the neighbours should come for the night to pray and to watch the dead. It kept all hands busy, and by midnight the room was so full of watchers that she could hardly provide enough to eat and to drink. For the richer a peasant is, the more neighbours come to the watching and praying by the corpse.

Wally looked on with silent aversion. Here lay a dead man—and so they ate and drank like so many flies! The dull hum and bustle were so strange to her after the sublime stillness of her mountain home, and struck her as so small and pitiful, that involuntarily she wished herself back again on the silent heights. Speechless and indifferent she passed to and fro between the noisy eating and drinking groups, and people said how much she resembled her dead father. On the third day was the funeral. From far and near people of the neighbouring hamlets came to it, partly to pay the last respect to the important and dreaded chief-peasant, partly to "make all straight" with the wicked Vulture-maiden, who now was mistress of all the great possessions of the Strommingers. Hitherto, indeed, she had been only an "incendiary" and a "ne'er do weel;" but now she was the wealthiest owner in all the mountain range, and that made all the difference.

Wally felt the change keenly, and she knew too whence it came. When she saw now after the funeral the same people stand before her with bent backs and obsequious grins, who, but one year before, had turned her from their doors with scorn and flouting when, starving with cold and hunger, she had asked them for work—then she turned away with loathing—then, and from that hour she despised mankind.

The curé of Heiligkreuz came too, and the Klötze from Rofen. Now was the moment for making at least an outward return for all their goodness to her when she had been poor and abandoned, and she distinguished them from all the others and kept with them only. When the funeral feast was over and the guests had at last dispersed, the priest of Heiligkreuz remained with her yet a little while, and spoke many good words to her. "Now you are mistress over many servants," he said, "but remember that he who does not know how to govern himself will not know how to govern others. It is an old saying, that 'he who cannot obey, cannot command'; learn to obey, my child, that you may be able to command."

"But, your reverence, whom am I to obey? There's no one here now that has any orders to give me."

"God."

Wally was silent.

"See here," said the curé, taking something from the pocket of his wide-skirted coat. "I have long meant this for you, ever since the time you were with me, but you could not have taken it with you in your wanderings." He took out of a box a small neatly-carved image of a saint with a little pedestal of wood.

"See, this is your patron saint, the holy Wallburga. Do you remember what I said to you about hard and soft wood, and about the good God who can carve a saint out of a knotty stick?"

"Yes, yes," said Wally.

"Well, you see, in order that you may not forget it, I have had a little image brought for me from Sölden. Hang it up over your bed, and pray before it diligently—that will do you good."

"I thank your reverence very much," said Wally, evidently delighted, as she took the fragile object carefully in her hard hands. "I will be sure always to remember when I look at it, how well you explained the meaning of it all to me. And this is how the holy Wallburga looked! Oh, she must indeed have been a sweet and lovely woman; but who could be so good and so pious as that?"

And as Klettenmaier came towards her across the courtyard, she held the figure out to him and cried, "See, Klettenmaier, what I have had given me; it is the holy Wallburga, my patron saint. We will send his reverence the first fine lamb that is dropped, as a present."

The good priest put in a sincere protest against this kind of return, but Wally, in her pleasure, paid no heed.

When the curé was gone, she went into her room and nailed the carved figure with the sacred images over her bed, and all round, like a wreath, she placed the pack of cards that had been old Luckard's. Then she went to see what there was to do in the farm or in the house.

"Hansl," she cried as she passed the vulture who was perched on the wood-shed, "*we* are the masters now!" And the sense of mastery after her long servitude pervaded her whole being, as intoxicating wine drunk in deep draughts fills the veins of an exhausted man.

In the courtyard the servants hired by Vincenz were all assembled, and Vincenz himself was amongst them. He had grown haggard, his face was of a yellow paleness, and on the back of his head in the midst of his thick black hair he had a bald place like a tonsure; his glaring eyes lay deep in their sockets, like the eyes of a wolf lurking in a crevice for his prey.

"What is it?" asked Wally, standing still. The upper servant, erewhile so rude, approached with timid subserviency.

"We only wished to ask thee if thou's meaning to send us away because we treated thee so badly while the master was alive? Thou knows we could only do what he would have done."

"You did only your duty," said Wally quietly. "I send none away unless I find him dishonest or a bad servant. And if you left off bowing and bending before me, you'd please me better. Go to your work that I may see what you can do, that's better worth than fooleries."

The people separated; Vincenz remained, his eyes fixed glowingly on Wally; she turned and stretched out her hand against him. "One only I banish from my hearth and home—thee, Vincenz," she said.

"Wally!" cried Vincenz, "this—this in return for all I did for thy father."

"What thou did for my father as his steward, so long as he was lame, that thou shall get a return for. I give thee the meadows that adjoin thy farm and round off thy land; that I think will repay thee thy time and trouble, and if not, say so—I'll be be-

holden to thee for nothing—ask what thou will—
but get thee from before my eyes."

"I want nought—I'll have nought but thee,
Wally. All is one to me without thee. Thou'st well
nigh murdered me, thou'st ill used me every time
I've ever seen thee—and—the devil's in it—I cannot
give thee up. Look here—I did it all for thee. For
thee I'd commit a murder—for thee I'd sell my soul's
salvation—and thou thinks to put me off with a
few meadows? Thou thinks to be free of me so?
Thou may offer me all thou hast—all thy land and
the Oetzthal into the bargain—I'd fling it back to
thee if thou didn't give me thyself. Look at me—
my very marrow is wasting away—I don't know how
it is, but for one single kiss from thee, I'd give thee
all my lands and goods and starve for the rest of
my days. Now send a clerk to reckon once again
with how many pounds and acres thou'll be rid of
me!" And with a glance of the wildest and bitterest
defiance at the astonished Wally he left the farm-
yard.

She was awed by him—she had never before
seen him thus; she had had a glimpse into the
depths of an unfathomable passion, and she wavered
between horror and pity.

"What is there in me," she thought, "that the
lads are all such fools about me?"

Ah, and only one came not; the only one that she would have had—despised her. And if—if meantime he were already married? The thought took away her breath. She thought again of the stranger that he had brought with him across the Hochjoch—but no—she was only a servant maid!

And yet something must happen soon! She was rich and important now, she might venture to take a step towards him! But all her maidenly pride stood in arms at the thought, and "Wait—wait," was still all that was left to her.

She felt driven restlessly through house and fields; soon it was apparent that she was spoilt for the village life; week followed week, and she could not accustom herself to it. She was and she remained the child of Murzoll—the wild Wally. She scorned pitilessly all that seemed to her petty or foolish, she could bind herself to no regularity, no customs, no habits. She feared no one—she had forgotten what fear was, up there on the Ferner, and she met the smaller life below with the same iron front that had defied the terrors of the elements. Mighty and strong of body and soul she stood among the villagers like a being of another world. She had become a stranger in the boorish herd who stared at her with distrust and dislike—as boors always stare at that which is unfamiliar—but who nevertheless dared not approach too near to the great proprietress. But the girl was sensible of their hostility, as of the mean cowardice which, while it spoke her fair to her face, betrayed its hatred behind her back.

"I ask leave of no one," was her haughty motto, and so she did whatever her wild spirit prompted. When she was in the humour, she would work all day like a labourer to incite the lazy servants, and if one of them was not up to the mark in his work, she would impatiently snatch it from his hand and do it herself. At other times she would spend the whole day in melancholy dreaming, or she would wander about the mountains so that people began to think her mind was unsettled. The men and maids meanwhile did as they pleased, and the neighbours maliciously whispered to each other that in this fashion she would let everything go to ruin.

While she thus set herself against all rule and order, she was on the other hand stern even to hardness in matters which the other peasants passed over much less strictly. If she detected a servant in dishonesty or false dealing she at once gave information to the justices. If any one ill-used a beast, she would seize him by the collar and shake him, beside herself with rage. If one of her people came home drunk in the evening, she would have him ignominiously locked out to pass the night out-of-doors, whether in rain or snow. If she discovered any immorality, the culprit that same hour was turned out of the house. For her spirit was chaste and pure as the glaciers with whom she had so long dwelt in solitude, and all the love-making and whispering, the meetings and serenadings that went on around her, filled her with horror.

All this gained her a reputation for unsparing hardness, and made her to be feared as her father had been before her.

Nevertheless she seemed to have bewitched all the young men. Not only her possessions;— no, she—she herself with all her strangeness was what the lads desired to win. When she stood before them, tall, as though standing on higher ground, slim and yet so strongly and proudly built that her close-laced boddice could hardly contain her nobly-moulded form, when she raised her arm, strong and nervous as a youth's, against them threateningly, whilst a lightning flash of scorn flamed like a challenge from her large black eyes— then a wild fire of love and strife seized the lads, and they would wrestle with her as if for life or death only to win a single kiss. But then woe to them, for they had not the strength to conquer this woman, and must go their way with scorn and derision. He was yet to come who alone could cope with her—would he ever come? Enough, she awaited him.

"He that can say of me I ever gave him a kiss, him will I marry, but he that's not strong enough to win that kiss by force—Wallburga Stromminger was not born for him!" she said haughtily one day, and soon the saying was reported in all the surrounding neighbourhood, and the young men came from far and near to try their luck and take her at her word. It became indeed a point of honour to be a suitor of the wild Wallburga, as any rash adventure is thought honourable by a man of strength and courage.

Soon there was not a man of marriageable age in all the three valleys who had not striven to conquer Wally and to wrest the kiss from her, but not one had succeeded. And she triumphed in the wild game and in her mighty strength, for she knew that she was talked of far and near, and that Joseph would often hear of her; and she thought that now he must at last think it worth the trouble to come and carry off the prize, it it were only to prove his strength—as that day when he had gone to slay the bear. If only he were here, she thought, why should

he not fall in love with her like all the others,—
above all, if she showed to him how sweet and
friendly she could be?

But he never came. Instead, there came one
day to the "Stag" which adjoined Wally's kitchen-
garden, the messenger from Vent. Wally, who was
at that moment weeding, heard Joseph's name
spoken and listened behind the hedge to the messenger's narration.

Since his mother's death Joseph Hagenbach goes
oftener to the "Lamb" at Zwieselstein—was the
man's story—and a love affair is talked about between him and the pretty Afra, the barmaid at the
"Lamb." Only yesterday he was up there, and
dined alone with Afra at the guest's table while the
hostess stayed in the kitchen. Suddenly the bull
broke loose, and ran through the village like a
whirlwind; a hornet had stung him in the ear. All
fled to their houses and shut to the doors, and the
innkeeper of the "Lamb" is about to do the same,
when he sees his youngest child, a girl of five, lying
in the road. She couldn't get up, for the children
had been playing coaches, and the little one was
harnessed to a heavy wheel-barrow when the cry
was raised that the bull was loose; the other children ran off, but little Liese with the heavy barrow
could not so quickly get away; she fell and en-

tangled herself in the rope, and there she lies right in the middle of the road, and the brute is snorting quite close to her with his horns lowered. There is no time to untie the child or to carry it off, barrow and all; the bull is there; the father and Afra scream so that they can be heard all through the village,—but all at once Joseph is on the spot, and thrusts a hay-fork into the side of the beast. The bull bellows and turns upon Joseph, and out of the windows, every one cries for help —but no one comes to help him. He seizes the bull by the horns, and with the strength of a giant forces him back a step or two whilst the bull struggles with him. Meanwhile the father has had time to fetch the child, and now the question is what will become of Joseph, whom all have left in the lurch? Afra wrings her hands and screams for help, the bull has forced Joseph with his horns to the ground and is about to trample on him, when from below Joseph strikes him in the neck with his knife, so that the blood spurts out all over him. The bull now begins to kick, lifting Joseph who holds tight on to his horns, then rushes furiously forward a little way, dragging Joseph with him, half in the air, and half on the ground: Joseph meanwhile, who wants to bring him to a stand-still again, never losing his hold. By this time the bull is bleeding from five wounds, and gradually getting weaker; once or twice Joseph finds his feet again, but each time the brute regains the mastery, and with desperate leaps hurries him on. The peasants have recovered themselves now and come out, the host of the "Lamb" at their head, to help Joseph with hay-forks and knives. But the bull hears the uproar behind him, and once more lowering his horns flings himself, with Joseph, against a closed barn door, so that every one thought Joseph must be crushed; but the door gives way under the blow and flies open, the bull rushes into the shed, and there wallows in his death-struggle among ladders, carts, and ploughs, so that all fall in confusion one over another. Joseph however swings himself up to a beam and throws the door to, so that the raging animal shall not get out again; the people outside hear him barricade the door; he is shut up in that narrow space alone with the brute, and those outside can do nothing. They hear the stamping and storming, the bellowing and uproar within, and shudder at the sound. At last all is still. After an anxious interval, the door is opened, and Joseph comes staggering forward bathed in blood and sweat. They suppose the bull is dead, but Joseph says it were a pity to kill so fine a beast, that his wounds

12*

could be healed and were none of them in a vital part.

In the barn all is in confusion, everything upset, trampled, and crushed, but the bull lies with all four legs tied and fastened to the floor; he lies motionless on his side, snorting and gasping, like a calf in a butcher's cart. Joseph has subdued the bull and bound him, alive—all by himself. There is no one like him.

When they came back with Joseph to the "Lamb," Afra fell on his neck before all the people, crying and sobbing, and the hostess brought Liese to him in her arms, and would have treated him to the best in the house—but Joseph was in no mood for any more merry-making. He drank one draught in his raging thirst, and then went home. The whole village was full of him, and that evening there was a great drinking-bout in his honour, that lasted far into the night.

This was the news the messenger brought from Vent, and again there was much talking about Joseph Hagenbach, and all the folks wondered that he should never come up here after Wally. The mistress of the Sonnenplatte had so many suitors—only Joseph seemed to wish to have nothing to do with her.

Wally left her place by the hedge: the words brought a hot blush of shame to her brow. Thus it was then that people spoke of her,—that Joseph would have nothing to say to her? And it was Afra that he was following? That was the same girl that he had brought with him over the Ferner the year before, and had been so careful of even then.

She sat down on a stone and covered her face with both hands. A storm raged within her, a storm of love, admiration, jealousy. Her heart was as though torn in pieces. She loved him—loved him as she had never done before, as though the panting breath with which she had followed the narration of his deed had fanned the glimmering spark into a glowing flame. Again, then—again he had done what no other could accomplish, but she had no part in it—for Afra's master it had been done, for love of Afra! Was it possible? must she give way to a maid-servant—she, the daughter of the Strommingers? Was not she the richest, and as all the young men told her, the most beautiful maid in all the land? Far and wide, was there one that could compare with her for strength and power? Was not she, and she alone, his equal, and should they two not come together? There was but the one Joseph in the world, and should he not belong to her? Should he throw himself away on Afra, on a miserable beggar girl? No, it could not be, it was impossible. Why, after all, should he not go to the Lamb, without its being for Afra's sake? He wandered about so much in the course of hunting, and the Lamb was at Zwieselstein, exactly where all the cross roads met. "O Joseph, Joseph, come to me," she moaned aloud, and threw herself with her face upon the ground, as if to cool its burning heat in the little dewy leaves. Then all at once she remembered how the messenger had said that Afra had thrown herself on Joseph's neck when he came back to the inn. She shuddered at the thought. And suddenly she pictured to herself how it would be if she were Joseph's wife, and if, when after such a struggle he came home weary, wounded, and bleeding, she had the right to receive him in her arms, to refresh him, to comfort him. How she would wash his hot brow and bind his wounds and lay him to rest on her heart till he fell asleep under her caresses! She had never thought of such things before, but now, as they crowded on her, she was thrilled by a hitherto unknown sense—as an open- ing flower trembles when it bursts the encasing bud.

In this moment she ripened into a woman, but, wild and ungovernable as all her feelings were, that which made her womanly stirred up all the hidden and sleeping powers of evil in her soul, and a fearful tempest raged within her.

The evening breeze swept coldly over her, she felt it not; night came on, and the ever-peaceful stars looked down with wondering eyes on the writhing form, as she lay on the earth in the night dews and tore her hair.

"The mistress wasn't in again all last night," said the housekeeper next morning to the underservants. "What is it, think you, that she does all night?" And they laid their heads together and whispered to each other.

But they all scattered like spray before the wind when Wally came towards them across the courtyard from the kitchen-garden; she was pale, and looked prouder and more imperious than ever. And so she continued; from that day forth she was changed, unjust, capricious, irritable, so that no one dared speak to her but old Klettenmaier, who always had more influence with her than any one else. And withal she carried her haughtiness in everything to the farthest point; her last word was always "the mistress"—for "the mistress" nothing was good enough—"the mistress" would not be pleased with this or with that—"the mistress" might permit herself things which no one else could venture on, and many another such provocation.

Every day she dressed herself as if it were Sunday, and had new clothes made, and even a silver necklace brought from Vent with all sorts of pendants in filigree-work, so heavy and costly that the like had never before been seen in the valley. At the feast of Corpus Christi she left off her mourning for her father and appeared in the procession so resplendent with silver and velvet and silk that the people could hardly say their prayers for gazing at her. It was the first time that she had joined in a procession, and indeed no one knew exactly what kind of a Christian she might be; but it was clear that she only went now to show her new clothes and her necklace, because most of the people of the canton from as far up as Vent, and as far down as Zwieselstein, were assembled there.

When she knelt down there was a rustling and jingling of stiff silks and plaitings and tinkling silver, and it seemed to say, "See, no one can have all this but the mistress of the Sonnenplatte!"

It happened that as the last Gospel was being read a slight confusion arose in the procession, and

some people who had been behind were now walking before her. They were the hostess of the Lamb
at Zwieselstein and the pretty slim Afra; she found
herself close to Wally, and nodded to her, then
looked back at Joseph, who was walking behind
with the men—so at least it seemed to Wally.
Afra looked so lovely at this instant, that for sheer
jealousy Wally forgot to return her salute. Then
she heard Afra say to her companion, "See there,
that is the Vulture-maiden, that let her vulture tear
Joseph to pieces nearly! Now she'll not even take
my good-day—and yet I've said many a Pater Noster
for her."

"Thou might have spared thyself the trouble
then," Wally broke in, "I want none to pray for
me—that I can do for myself."

"But as it seems to me, thou doesn't do it,"
retorted Afra.

"I've no need to pray as much as other folk;
I've enough and to spare, and don't need to
pray to God like a poor maid-servant, who must
say a Pater Noster whenever she's in want of a new
shoe-ribbon."

The angry blood mounted in Afra's face. "Oh,
for that matter, a shoe-ribbon that's been prayed
for may bring more happiness than a silver
necklace that's been got in a godless way."

"Yes, yes," said the hostess, putting in her word, "Afra's in the right there."

"If my necklace doesn't please thee, walk behind me, then thou'll not see it; nor does it become the mistress of the Sonnenplatte to walk behind a servant wench."

"It'd do thee no harm to tread in Afra's footsteps—that I tell thee plainly," retorted the innkeeper's wife.

"Shame on you, hostess, to lower yourself by taking part with your own maid," cried Wally with flashing eyes. "He who doesn't value himself, none other will value!"

"Oh! then a maid-servant's not a human soul!" said Afra, trembling from head to foot. "A silk gown though, makes no difference to the good God; He sees what's beneath it, a good heart or a bad!"

"Yes, truly," cried Wally with an outbreak of hatred, "it's not every one can have so good a heart as thine—above all towards the lads. Go to the Devil!"

"Wally!" exclaimed Afra, and the tears rushed from her eyes. But she had to be silent, for at this moment the procession had again reached the church, the last benediction was pronounced,

and the procession broke up. Wally shot by
Afra like a queen, so that she had to cling to
her companion; she had almost run over the
girl, and every one turned to look after her. The
men said no more beautiful maid was to be found
in all the Tyrol, but the women were bursting
with envy.

"She looks rather different now to what she did
up on the Hochjoch, with a dog's hole to live in
and neither combed nor coiffed—like a wild thing!"
said Joseph, who was standing not far off, and
looked at her with wondering eyes; then he nodded
a farewell to Afra, and quitted the crowd; he wanted
to be home by midday.

But Afra hastened after Wally. Her pretty blue
eyes sparkled with tears, like water sprinkled on a
fire; she was beside herself with anger, and so was
the innkeeper's wife. They caught up Wally at
the village inn. She too was in the most terrible
agitation; she had seen the affectionate familiar
farewell that Joseph had nodded to Afra, and to
her—to her, as she believed—he had not vouchsafed a single glance. And now he was gone, and
all the hopes betrayed that she had set on this
day's doings. This Afra! all her anger was centered
on her, she could have trampled her under foot.
And here was Afra standing before her, stopping

her way and speaking to her with angry defiance—
she, the low servant-girl!

"Mistress," Afra brought out breathlessly,
"thou's said a thing that I cannot let pass, for it
touches my character—what did thou mean by
saying I had a good heart towards the lads? I
will know what lay behind those words!"

"Dost wish to make a quarrel with Wallburga Stromminger," cried Wally, and her flashing eyes looked straight down upon the girl.
"Dost think I'd enter into strife with such a one as
thou?"

"With such a one as me," cried the girl, "what
sort of one am I then? I'm a poor maid and
have had none to care for me, but I've done no
one any harm, nor set fire to any one's house.
I've no need to put up with anything from *thee*—
know that."

Wally started as though stung by a snake.

"A wench art thou, a shameless servant wench
that throws thyself on a lad's neck before every
one," she cried, forgetting herself and every thing,
so that the people crowded round her.

"What? who? whose neck?" stammered the girl,
turning pale.

"Shall I tell thee? Shall I?"

"Yes, speak out; I have a good conscience, and the mistress of the Lamb here, she can testify that it is not true."

"Indeed—not true! is it not true that two years ago, when thou hardly knew Joseph, he dragged thee with him over the Hochjoch, and had to carry thee half the way because thou made as though thou could walk no farther? Is it not true thou'st never let him be since, so that everyone names him and thee together? Is it not true thou keeps Joseph away from other maids that have better right and were better wives for him than thou—a vagabond serving-girl? Is it not true that only the other day, when he had fought the bull, thou fell on his neck before the whole village as if thou'd been his promised wife? Is none of that true?"

Afra covered her face with her hands, and wept aloud, "Oh, Joseph, Joseph, that I should have to put up with this."

"Be quiet, Afra," said the good natured land-lady consolingly, "she has betrayed herself, it's only her anger because Joseph doesn't run after her and won't burn his fingers for her like the other lads. If only Joseph were here he would make her tell a different story."

"Yes, I can well believe that he wouldn't leave his pretty sweetheart in the lurch," said Wally, with a laugh so terribly sharp and shrill that the sound re-echoed from the hills like a cry of pain. "Such a sweetheart, who hangs about his neck, is no doubt more convenient than one who must first be won, and with whom it might come to pass that he'd have to take himself off again with scorn and mockery. The proud bear-hunter would no doubt sooner mate with such a one than with the Vulture-Maiden!"

The innkeeper now stepped forward. "Hearken," he said, "I've had enough of this; the lass is a good lass—my wife and I, we answer for her, and we'll let no harm come to her. Do thou take back thy words; I order it—dost understand?"

Again Wally laughed aloud, "Landlord," she said. "Did thou ever hear tell that the Vulture lets itself be ordered by the Lamb?"

Everyone laughed at the play of words, for the host of the Lamb was proverbially called a "Lamperl,"* because he was a weak good-natured man who would put up with anything.

"Aye, thou deserves thy name, thou Vulture-Wally—that thou dost."

* Lamb.

"Make way there," Wally now exclaimed, "I've had enough of this—this threshing of empty straw. Let me pass!" and she would have pushed Afra on one side under the doorway.

But the innkeeper's wife held Afra by the arm.

"Nay, thou's no call to make way—get thee in first; thou'rt no worse than she is," she said, as she tried to press through the door with Afra in front of Wally.

Wally seized Afra by the waist, lifted her up and flung her from the door into the arms of the nearest bystander. "First come the mistresses, and after them the maids," she said; then passing before everyone into the room she seated herself at the head of the table.

Everyone chuckled and clapped their hands at the audacious jest. Afra cried and was so abashed that she would not go in, and the innkeeper and his wife took her home.

"Only wait, Afra," said the good woman consolingly on the way home, "I'll send Joseph to her, and he will take her in hand." But Afra only shook her head and said no one would do her any good; disgraced she was, and disgraced she must remain.

"Well, but why must thou needs begin a quarrel

with that bad girl of Stromminger's," said the land-lord, scolding her good-naturedly, "every one keeps out of her way that can."

Meanwhile Wally sat within and looked out of window at Afra departing with her companions; her heart beat so that the silver pendants to her neck-lace tinkled softly.

She was called upon to eat, the vermicelli soup was getting cold; but she found the soup bad and the mutton as tough as leather; she tossed a gulden on the table, would take no change, and in the face of all the astonished peasants rustled out of the house.

Just as she had done after her confirmation five years before, she tore off her fine clothes when she got home, and flung them into the chest. The silver necklace with its filigree work she trampled into a shapeless mass. What good had her splendour done her? It had not helped her to please the only one whom she desired to please. And, as once before, she threw herself on her bed, angrily chafing against the holy images. A piercing torment tortured her soul as if with knives. Her eyes fell on the carved image of Wallburga above her, and then she thought that the pain she was enduring might be the knife of God working on her, to make out of her a Saint—as the curé had said. But why should she be made a saint? She would so much rather be a happy woman. And that might have been done so easily; the good God would not have needed to carve her out for that—she would already have been quite right just as she was!

So she murmured and rebelled against the knife of God.

———

CHAPTER XI.

At Last.

FOR some time Wally's moods had been almost unendurable. The whole night through she would wander about in the open air; by day she was full of unceasing and indomitable energy, labouring restlessly early and late, and expecting every one else to do the same—an impossibility for most people. Vincenz might now venture to call again, for he always knew the latest news in the valley— and Wallburga had all at once grown eager for news. When Vincenz perceived this, he made it his express business to enquire far and near, so as always to have some new thing to retail to Wally, who thus became gradually accustomed to see him every day. He soon observed that she always showed more curiosity about Sölden and Zwiesel-stein than about any other place, and cunning as he was, he easily discovered the reason. He con-stantly brought word of the continued intimacy between Joseph and Afra; it was news that threw Wally into the most frightful agitation, but he feigned not to perceive this, and cautiously avoiding any mention of his own love, succeeded in making her feel secure and trustful with him. But he was consumed with jealousy of Joseph; that Hagenbach was the curse of his life. There was no glory in which he had not anticipated him, no deed of valour in which he had not stood before him, no match at skittles or at shooting at which he had not carried off the prize, and now he had taken from him Wally's heart also—Wally's heart, which his persistent suit might perhaps have won, had not Joseph been there. "Why does God Almighty pour everything down on one man and deal so niggardly with another?" growled Vincenz, and tormented himself secretly as much as Wally did. If they had only done their lamentations and grumbling together, it would have been enough to desolate the whole Oetz valley!

One evening—it was in haytime—Wally was helping to load a large hay-cart; the load was ready and only the great crossbar had to be set in its place, but the hay was piled so high that the men could not throw it across. When they had got it half way up, they let it slip again, laughing and playing foolish tricks the while. Wally's patience all at once gave way. "Get out, you blockheads," she exclaimed, and mounted on the waggon, pushing the men to right and left out of her way; then drawing in the rope, she pulled up the crosstree, seized hold of one end of it with both her rounded arms, and with a single jerk hoisted it on to the waggon. A shout of admiration broke from all; the girls laughed at the men for not being able to do what a woman had done, and the men scratched their heads and thought that all could not be as it should be with the mistress, and that the devil must have a hand in it.

Wally stood on the waggon, and looked at the red setting sun. In her attitude and on her features was an expression of proud satisfaction; once more she had felt the certainty that not one was her equal, and strong in her sense of power, she was ready to challenge the whole world.

At that moment Vincenz came up. "Wally," he called out to her, "thou looks like Queen Potiphar on the elephant. If Joseph had seen Potiphar like that, for certain he'd not have been so bashful."

Wally turned crimson at these offensive words, and sprang down from the waggon. "I forbid such jests with me," she said, when she was on the ground.

"Nay," disclaimed Vincenz, "I meant no harm; but thou looked so handsome up there, it came out without thinking: it shall not happen again."

They walked on silently together.

"What news is stirring?" asked Wally at last, according to custom.

"Not much," said Vincenz; "they say that Hagenbach is going to take the maid Afra to the dance at Sölden on St. Peter's Day. I heard it from the messenger who had had to fetch a new pair of shoes from Imst for Afra, and a silk neckerchief, and Joseph paid for them." Wally bit her lips and said nothing, but Vincenz saw what was passing in her mind.

"I tell thee what," said Vincenz, "we also do things in style on St. Peter's Day, and if the peasant-mistress would come, there would be a feast to be talked of far and wide; come for once with me to the dance."

Wally gave her head a short toss. "I'm the right sort to go to dances," she said.

"Nay go, Wally," urged Vincenz, "just for once, if it's only to spite people."

"Much I care for them," said Wally, laughing contemptuously.

"But think a bit, people say—" he paused.

Wally stood still. "What do they say?" she asked, looking at him piercingly.

Vincenz shrank back at the expression on her countenance. "I only mean that they say thou's got some secret trouble. The upper servant says thou wast out the whole night, and goes wandering about like a sick chicken. And folk say thou'st everything heart can desire, and suitors as many as the sand on the seashore, so if thou's not content with that, there must be some love-sorrow on thy mind—and ever since what happened at the Procession—"

"Well! go on!" said Wally huskily.

"Since then they say that Joseph is the only lad in the Oetz valley that thou cares to catch—and that he won't bite."

He darted a lightning glance at Wally as he said the words; they touched her to the quick. She had to stand still and lean her forehead against the trunk of a tree, the blood throbbed so in her temples.

"And if it is so, if they do say such things behind my back—" she gasped, but she could not finish; a sudden mist seemed to cloud and confuse all her thoughts.

Vincenz gave her time to recover herself; he knew what it must be to her, for he knew her pride. After a time he said,

"Look here, it seems to me thou'd best come with me to the dance; that were the best way to stop peoples' mouths."

Wally drew herself up. "I go with no lad to the dance that I don't mean to marry—that I tell thee once for all!" she said.

"If I was thee, I'd sooner marry Vincenz Gellner than die an old maid for love of Hagenbach," said Vincenz sneeringly.

Wally looked at him with newly-awakened aversion. "I wonder thou'rt not tired of that," she said; "when thou knows well it's all of no good."

"Wally, I ask thee for the last time, can thou not bring thyself to think of me as a husband?"

"Never—never! sooner will I die," she said.

Vincenz' sharp and prominent cheek bones-became white spots on his yellow face; he looked almost like the vulture, glancing sideways at Wally, as at some defenceless prey. "I'm sorry, Wally," he said, "but I've somewhat to say to thee—something that I'd fain have spared thee, but thou forces me to it. I've given thee a twelvemonth, and now I must speak." He drew a written sheet of paper from his pocket. "It's nigh upon a year since thy father died, and if thou doesn't marry me at the year's end thy right to the farm is over."

Wally stared at him.

He unfolded the paper. "Here's thy father's

will, by which he appoints that if thou don't marry me by a twelvemonth after his death, the farm and all belonging to it is mine, and thou gets no more than he was bound by law to leave thee. There'll be an end then of the proud peasant-mistress. As yet, no one knows of this. Thou can turn it over once more, and in the end I fancy thou'll give in, sooner than go with me before the justices, and have the will carried out."

Wally stood still, and measured Vincenz from head to foot with a single glance of cold contempt, then said with perfect calmness: "Oh thou pitiful fool! In *this* net then thou'st thought to catch the Vulture-maiden? You are a pair, thou and my father, but neither one nor the other of you knew me. What do I care for money or property? That which I want cannot be bought with gold, and so I care nothing for it. On Monday will I pack up my things, and go away again, for thy guest I'll never be—no, not for an hour. And if it gives me pain to leave this farm, where I first saw the light—still, I've been no happier as mistress than when I minded the cattle—and as much a stranger here as there. So it's all for the best, and I'll leave the place, and go away as far as I can."

Calmly she turned towards the house. A wild

anguish seized Vincenz; he threw himself at her feet, and clasped her knees. "I never meant that," he cried, "thou mustn't go away,—for God's sake, don't serve me so—what do I want with the farm? I only meant—my God, my God—only to try everything!" With one hand he held Wally fast, with the other he thrust the paper into his mouth, and tore it with his teeth. "There, there, see, there goes the scrawl—I'll have none of the farm, if thou'll not stay—there—there—" he strewed the fragments to the wind, "I want nothing—nothing— only don't thou serve me so—don't go away!"

Wally looked at him in wonder. "I pity thee, Vincenz, but I cannot help thee—no more than I myself am helped. Keep thou the farm and all that belongs to it; my father left it to thee, and that remains the same, although thou hast torn up the will—I'll take nothing as a gift from thee. Everything here is hateful to me, even now— why should I wait? No one is any good to me, nor I to any one. I'll take my Hansl, and go up again to the mountain—that is where I belong. But if I might ask thee one thing—tell no one till I'm gone that the farm was never mine; for thou seest—there's one thing I cannot bear—that folk should make fun of me. That—that drives me mad. Think of the pointing, and the scorn when they know that the proud Wally Stromminger has been turned out of house and home like a maid-servant—I couldn't live through it. Let me at least go forth as mistress."

"Wally," cried Vincenz, "where thou goest, I will go. Thou cannot hinder me—the roads are free to all, and he who will, may run. If thou'rt resolved to leave—I go with thee."

Wally looked at him with amazement, as he stood there raving before her, and she shuddered as though she had raised some evil spirit. "What will come of it all?" she murmured helplessly.

At this moment the messenger from Sölden was seen coming across the meadows from the house straight towards Wally. He had a big nosegay in his hat and in his Sunday-coat, like a bridal messenger.

"He's come to bid thee to Joseph and Afra's wedding," cried Vincenz with a wild laugh. Wally's foot stumbled against something; she caught hold of Vincenz, and he seized her round the waist and held her.

Meanwhile the messenger came up, and took off his hat to Wally. "Good day to thee, Mistress. Joseph Hagenbach sends thee friendly greeting, and asks thee to the dance on St. Peter's Day. If it's thy pleasure, he will come up at noon and fetch thee down to the Stag. Thou'lt send an answer by me."

If Heaven itself had opened before Wally, and Hell before Vincenz, it would have been much the same thing.

Then it was not true about Afra! He had come to Wally—he had come after five years of sorrow and suffering — at last, at last! The word was spoken—the winds bore it triumphantly onwards, the breezes echoed it back again, the white glaciers smiled at it in the evening sunshine; Joseph the Bear-hunter bade the Vulture-maiden to the dance! The labourers in the field shouted, the waggons swayed beneath their loads, the vulture on the roof flapped his wings for joy—the two who belonged to one another were come together at last!

Joy to all mankind: the race of giants would live again in this one pair. And smiling graciously, like a Queen beneath the myrtle crown, Wally bowed her beautiful head and told the messenger, half-bashfully, that she should expect Joseph.

Vincenz leaned against a tree, distorted, faded, mute—a ghost of the past.

Wally threw him a compassionate glance—he was no longer to be dreaded: she bore a charmed life, none could hurt or harm her more. She hastened into the house, and the servants looked at her wonderingly, such rapture lay in her expression. But she could not stay indoors; she took money, and went through the village like a bliss-bestowing fairy. She entered all the poorest huts, and gave with liberal hand out of that which she could rightfully and lawfully call her own,* for she had decided irrevocably that the farm should belong to Vincenz. She was still rich enough to give to Joseph, and to all around her—even her rightful share of Stromminger's estate was a fortune. She must do good to all; she could not bear alone her newly-learnt, immeasurable happiness.

The two days before St. Peter's festival were like a fairy tale to all the villagers. Who could now recognize the morose and bitter Vulture-maiden in the beatified girl who moved about as though borne on invisible wings? It had needed but this one ray of sunshine, and the hail-stricken, frost-bitten blossom had sprung up again. An inexhaustible power made itself felt in her bosom, a power for love as for hatred, for joy as for pain, for self-sacrifice as for defiance. All around her breathed more freely; it was as though a spell had been taken off them since Wally's dark repining

---

* In most foreign countries the law provides that a certain portion of a man's estate is inalienable from his natural heirs.

spirit, that had weighed like a storm-cloud upon everything, had melted away.

"When one is as happy as I am, every one else should rejoice too," she said; and soon it was known everywhere that it was because Joseph had asked her to the dance—which was almost the same as asking her in marriage—that Wally was so changed. Why should she conceal it, when in so few days it would be known? why should she deny that she loved him with all her heart, above everything? he deserved it all, and he loved her in return, or he would not be coming to fetch her to the dance. It was well for her that she dared to show all that she felt. If she met a child she took it in her arms, and told it how, on St. Peter's Day, Joseph the bear-hunter was coming—Joseph, who had slain the great bear, and saved the innkeeper's little Lieserl from the mad bull, and how they would all open their eyes, he was so tall, and so beautiful to look at—they had never seen such a man, for there was not such another in all the wide world. The children were quite excited, and played all day at Bear and Joseph the bear-hunter. Then she joked with Hansl, threatening him playfully. "Thou'rt to behave thyself when Joseph comes, else something will happen—that I can tell thee!" and Klettenmaier and all the best of the servants had

new holiday-clothes — they knew well enough the
reason why; but Wally let them chatter as they
would about it, and was not angry.

Then again she would sit for hours quietly in
her room, doing nothing, wondering only how it
had happened that Joseph had so suddenly changed
his mind; but however much she thought and
thought she could not understand why the unhoped-
for happiness, so sudden, so full, so complete, had
come upon her; and she looked up at her holy
images, no longer with enmity, but with friendly
eyes, and thanked them for all the good that they
had brought to her. But when she looked at the
cards that were nailed up above her bed, she
laughed aloud. "Well, what do you now say?
Own that you knew nothing of what was coming!"
and like enchanted spirits that no liberating spell
can call forth again into the light, the secrets of
the future stared unintelligibly at her from these
mute tokens. If only old Luckard had been there,
she could have told what it was the cards replied
to Wally—but to her they were dumb, like a cipher
of which the key is lost. If Luckard had been alive,
how rejoiced she would have been! Wally would
have liked to lie down and sleep till the day of the
festival, so that the time might not appear so long.
But there was no question of sleep; she could not

even close an eye by day or by night for impatience. She was always counting, "Now so many hours more—now so many—"

At last the day was come. After breakfast Wally went to her room, and washed herself, and combed her hair without end. Once more she was a woman—a girl! Once more she stood before the glass, and adorned herself, and looked to see if she were fair, if she might hope to find favour in Joseph's eyes; and once more she had procured a new necklace, even more beautiful than the first, and filigree pins for her hair as well. The box was on the table before her, she took out the ornament, and tied it above her bodice; the bright silver was as white as the snowy pleated sleeves of her chemise and tinkled like clear marriage-bells, and through the rose-coloured chintz curtains a dim rosy light shed a tender mist of bridal-glow over the girl's noble figure. When she was ready, she took from its case a meerschaum pipe heavy with silver, such as no peasant of the country had far and wide—a really splendid pipe—and yet she held it long in her hand, doubting whether it were good enough for Joseph. And still there was something else, that she took out slowly, almost timidly, looking at the door to see if it were securely fastened; it was a small round box, and in it there lay—a ring. She trembled as she took it out, and a tear of unutterable joy and thankfulness glistened in her eye. She held the ring in her folded hands, and for the first time for many days she knelt down, and she prayed over it that the beloved one might be linked to her for ever. And she no longer heard the rustle of her silks, and the tinkle of her silver ornaments; she was lost in the passionate fervour of her prayers; she pressed forward as it were to the presence of God with the vehemence of a thankful child whose father has granted its warmest desire.

"The mistress will never have done with dressing herself to-day," said the maids outside, as Wally did not appear.

Already the peasants were flocking to the Stag. Whoever had feet to go on, and Sunday-clothes to go in, would be there to-day, for the whole village was stirred by the great event of the peasant-mistress going to the dance with Joseph Hagenbach. The road swarmed with people, and the landlord of the Stag had done his best, and sent for musicians to come from Imst.

The upper maid-servant stood at the dormer-window above, and looked down the road by which Joseph must come. Wally stood ready dressed in her room; her heart beat like a sledge-hammer, her cheeks glowed, her hands were icy-cold, she held her white neatly-folded handkerchief pressed tightly to her heart—it had been her mother's wedding handkerchief. The pipe and the ring for Joseph she had hidden away in her pocket; so she waited motionless whilst the minutes passed by, and this silent pause of expectation, in which her breath almost failed her for impatience, was certainly one of the hardest experiences of her life.

"They're coming, they're coming!" cried the maid at last. "Joseph and a crowd of other lads from Zwieselstein and Sölden, and the landlord of the Lamb—it's a regular procession!"

Everyone ran out into the courtyard; already the noise of the approaching steps and voices could be heard in Wally's room. She came out, and a general "Ah!" of admiration broke from all as she appeared.

At the same moment the procession approached the farm-gate, Joseph at its head. She went forward to meet him, modestly but with the beaming loftiness of a bride who is proud of her bridegroom—proud to have been chosen by such a man.

"Joseph, art thou there?" she said, and her voice sounded soft and loving as she had never spoken before. Joseph glanced at her with a strange, almost a shamefaced look, and then cast his eyes down again.

Wally was startled—was it on purpose, or was it by accident? Joseph had placed his black-cock feather upside down, as the young men are in the habit of doing when they seek a quarrel. It could only have happened from an oversight to-day!

Every one stood round and watched her; she was so anxious that she could say no more, and he also was silent. She looked at him with eyes full of fervent moisture, but his avoided hers. He was as much embarrassed as she was, she thought.

"Come," he said at last, and offered his hand. She laid hers in it, and they silently walked as far as the Stag. The strangers and all the servants closed the procession.

As, sometimes, when we have gazed at the sun, all grows black before us, even in full daylight, so now with Wally in the midst of her happiness, all suddenly grew dark to her soul. She knew not how it was; she was bewildered and hardly knew herself—it was all so different from what she had imagined.

A noisy countrydance was beginning as they entered the Stag, and as Wally passed down the long rows of dancers with Joseph, she heard the people say: "There is not a handsomer couple in the whole world." She now saw for the first time how many strangers had come with Joseph, and that all her rejected suitors were there also. Once more she silently compared them with Joseph, and she could truly say there was not one of them who came up to him for stature and beauty. He was a king among the peasants, a mortal of quite another stamp to the ordinary men who stood around him, and her eye rested with silent delight on the tall figure, from his broad chest down to his slender knees and ankles. Any one seeing him thus must surely understand that him only would she have, and none other.

As she looked round, her glance met two piercing black eyes directed like daggers at Joseph. It was Vincenz, wedged in among the crowd. And not far off was another melancholy face—that of Benedict Klotz, who observed her thoughtfully. As she passed him, he pulled her gently back by the sleeve. "Mind what thou'rt about, Wally," he whispered, "there's some plot against thee—I don't know what, but I forebode no good."

Wally shrugged her shoulders carelessly. What harm could happen to her, when Joseph was at her side?

14*

The sets formed for the dance, and Joseph and
Wally were to begin; every one wanted to see
them dance together. No couple had yet been
watched with such envious eyes as this well-
dressed, distinguished-looking pair. Joseph, however, moved away from Wally's side, and stood
before her with something of solemnity in his
air.

"Wally," he said aloud, and the music stopped
at a sign from the host of the Lamb, who stood
behind them, "I hope that before we dance together, thou'lt give me the kiss that no one of thy
suitors has yet been able to win from thee?"

Wally coloured and said softly, "But not here
Joseph, not before everyone."

"Precisely here, before everyone," said Joseph,
with strong emphasis.

For a moment Wally struggled between desire
and sweet embarrassment; to kiss a man before all
these people was to her chaste and half-defiant
spirit a severe humiliation. But there he stood before her, the man so dear to her heart; the moment
for which she would joyfully have given a year of
her life—nay her life itself—was there, and should
she reject it for the sake of a few bystanders who
could do her no harm, if she did kiss her bridegroom? She raised her beautiful face to his, and

his eyes were fixed for a moment on the full and blooming lips that approached his own. Then with an involuntary movement, he pushed her gently from him, saying softly,

"Nay, not so; a true hunter shoots his game only on the spring or on the wing—that I told thee once before. The kiss I'll wrest from thee, not take it as a gift. And were I a maid like thee, I'd give myself away less cheaply. Defend thyself, Wally, that I may win no easier than the others, else my honour is lost."

A scarlet blush overspread Wally's face; she could have sunk into the ground for shame. Had she then so completely forgotten what she owed to herself, that her lover must remind her of it? She was crimson to her very eyes—it was as though a wave of blood were surging to her brain. Drawing herself up to her full height, with one flaming glance she measured herself with him. "Good," she said, "thou shalt have thy will—thou also shalt learn to know the Vulture-maiden. Look to thyself, whether now thou'lt get the kiss!"

She was almost suffocated. She tore off her neckerchief and stood there in her silver-clasped velvet bodice and white linen chemise, so that Joseph's eyes rested in amazement on her beautiful bare neck. "Thou'rt handsome—as handsome as thou'rt wicked," he muttered, and springing on her, as a hunter springs on a wild animal to give the death-blow, he threw his strong arms round her neck. But he did not know the Vulture-maiden. With one powerful wrench she was free, and there was a laugh of derision from all those with whom it had fared no better, that maddened Joseph. He seized her round the waist with arms of iron, but she struck him such a blow on the heart, that he cried out and staggered backwards. Renewed laughter! With this blow, of which she knew the value, she had always defended herself against her importunate suitors, for none had held out after it. But Joseph smothered his pain, and with redoubled fury threw himself again on the girl, seized her by the arms with both hands, and so tried to approach her lips; but in an instant she bent herself down on one side, and now ensued a breathless struggle up and down, to and fro, an oppressive silence broken only by an occasional oath from Joseph. The girl bowed and twisted herself hither and thither like a snake in his arms, so that he could never reach her mouth. It was no longer a strife for love—it was a struggle for life and death. Three times he had got her down to the ground, three times she sprang up again; he lifted her in his arms, but she always twisted herself round, and he could not touch her lips. Her fine linen hung in rags, her silver necklace was all broken to pieces. Suddenly she freed herself, and flew to the doorway; he overtook her, and like a stormwind tore her back into his arms. It was a fierce and glowing embrace. His breath floated round her like hot steam; she lay on his breast; she felt his heart beat against her own; her strength left her, she fell on her knees before him, and said, as if fainting with pain, and shame, and love, "Thou hast me!"

"Ah!" a heavy sigh broke from Joseph. "You have all of you seen it?" he asked aloud—he bent down and pressed his mouth upon her hot and quivering lips. A loud hurrah filled the room. She got up and sank almost senseless on his breast.

"Stay!" he said in a hard voice, and stepped back a little, "ONE kiss is enough—no need of more. Thou'st seen now that I can master thee—and no further will I go."

Wally stared at him, as if she could not understand his words. She was of an ashy paleness.

"Joseph," she stammered, "why then art thou come?"

"Didst think I had come to woo thee?" he answered. "Lately at the procession thou'st said before everyone that Afra was my sweetheart, because she was so easy to be had,—and that Joseph the bear-slayer had not the heart to try and win the Vulture-Wally. Didst truly think a lad with any spirit in him would let such things be said of him and of an honest girl? I only wished to show thee that I can master thee as I can a bear, or a mad bull, and the kiss I have won frcm thee, that will I take to Afra, as a kiss of atonement for the wrong that thou hast done her. Now take heed to thyself another time when thy haughty temper moves thee. Henceforth, perhaps, thou'll forego the pleasure of holding up a poor and honest girl to scorn and derision—now that thou'st felt what it is to be a laughing-stock thyself."

A shout of laughter from all sides closed Joseph's speech, but he turned with displeasure from the applause. "You have seen that I've kept my word," he said, "and now I must go to Zwieselstein to comfort Afra. The good soul wept to think that I should play the peasant-mistress such a shabby trick. God keep you all."

He went, but they all ran after him; it had been too good a joke. Joseph was something like a man. He had shown the proud peasant-mistress that she had a master.

"It will do her good!"

"It will serve her right!"

"Joseph, that's the best day's work thou's ever done."

"No one'll have anything to do with her, when this is known."

Thus laughed the chorus of rejected suitors, as they crowded joyfully round Joseph.

The dancing-floor was deserted — only two persons remained with Wally, Vincenz and Benedict. Wally stood still in the same place and did not stir; it was as if she were lifeless.

Vincenz watched her with folded arms. Benedict went up to her and took her gently by the arm. "Wally, don't take it so to heart—we are here, and we'll get satisfaction for thee. Wally— speak. What shall we do? we are all ready, only say what thou'd have us to do."

Then she turned round, her large eyes had a ghostly gleam in them, her face was ghastly pale. She opened and closed her lips once or twice, one word there was she struggled to utter, but it seemed as if the breath to speak it failed her. At last she brought it out, as from the very depths of her being,—more a cry than a word: "DEAD would I have him!"

Benedict drew back. "God forbid, Wally!" he said.

But Vincenz stepped forward with flashing eyes. "Wally, art thou in earnest?"

"Ay, in bloody earnest!" She lifted her hand at the oath, her hand was quite stiff and the nails blue, as in one dead. "He who lays him dead at his Afra's feet—him will I marry, as truly as I am Wallburga Stromminger."

CHAPTER XII.

In the Night.

ALL through the night a strange and measured sound was audible throughout the silent, sleeping farm-house. Now and then the maids awoke and listened, without knowing what they heard, then turned to sleep again. The boards cracked and the beams trembled, slightly but unceasingly.

It was Wally who paced backwards and forwards with heavy, unpausing steps, her sinking heart engaged in a death-struggle with herself, with Fate, with Providence. All around was shattered —her clothes flung about the room, on the floor the carved St. Wallburga, the crucifix, the holy images, all broken to fragments in impotent wrath.

She had half-undressed, and her hair fell loose and disordered on her bare shoulders. A red gleaming pine-torch flickered in its socket, and in the trembling shadows the features of the broken figure of Christ looking distorted and living. She stayed her steps, and looked down on the fragments.

"Ay, thou may grin," she said, "thou's always taken me for a fool. You're of no good, none of you; idols you are of wood and paper, and no help to any one. Neither prayer nor curse can you hear. And them for whom you stand, hide themselves, God knows where, and would laugh if they could see how we kneel down before a piece of wood." And she pushed the fragments under the bed, that they might not be in her way as she walked to and fro.

A shot was heard in the distance.

Wally stood still and listened; all was silent. She must have fancied it. Why should the sound have taken her breath away? She was not even sure that it was a shot. The thought flashed through her like lightning, "Suppose Vincenz should have shot Joseph!" It was mere folly, Joseph was safe at home —or perhaps at Zwieselstein with his Afra!

She beat her head against the wall in nameless agony at the thought, and pictures rose before her that drove her frantic. If only he were dead—dead so that she need never think of him again! She flung the window open that she might breathe more freely.

Hansl, who was asleep on a tree outside the window, woke up and fluttered in half-stupid with sleep. "Ah, thou!" cried Wally, and stretched out her arms to him; she clasped him to her breast, he was all—all that was left to her in the world.

Again—a second shot, and this time distinctly in the direction of Zwieselstein; she let go of the vulture, and pressed her hand to her heart, as though she herself had been struck. Why this terror? The trifling incident had suddenly brought before her the whole terrible deed which yesterday she had sworn to. She could not help thinking again and again how it would be if the shot she had just heard had shattered Joseph's head, and a wild and frenzied joy came upon her. Now he belonged to her only, now none other could claim his kiss, and as she thought upon it, it seemed to her as though it had really happened; she saw him lying on the ground in his blood, she knelt down by him, she took his head in her lap, she kissed the pale face—the beautiful pale face—she saw it actually before her. And then suddenly pity overwhelmed her for the poor, dead man, a burning, unutterable pity; she called him by every loving name, she shook him, she chafed his hands —in vain, he was no more. Unspeakable anguish filled her soul; no, this must not be, he must not die—sooner would she part with her own life!

She felt as if an icy cramp had been grasping and crushing her heart, so that no warm human blood could flow in her veins, and that now the grip was at last relaxed and the hot flood streaming into her heart again. She must go out, she must see whether

Vincenz was at home, she must speak to him at once, before daybreak, she must tell him that the ghastly deed must not be done—she was in a fever, all her pulses throbbed. She had desired the deed, commanded it, but already the idea that it might have been done, extinguished her wrath—and she forgave.

She threw a neckerchief on her shoulders, and hastened across the courtyard and through the garden to Vincenz' house. What would he, what would everyone think of her? It was all one—what did it matter now?

She reached the house. There was a light in Vincenz' room on the groundfloor; noiselessly she glided up, she could see through the parted curtains —her heart stood still—the room was empty, the pine-torch almost burnt away. She went round the house; the door was unfastened, she opened it softly and went in. All was still as death, the men and maids fast asleep; she crept through the whole house, nothing stirred—Vincenz was away! The blood curdled in her veins; she went into his bedroom, the bed was disturbed—he must have laid himself down, then risen again; his Sunday clothes were hanging up, but his work-day clothes were missing, nor was his hat in its place. She looked into the sitting-room; the nail where his rifle usually hung was empty.

Wally stood as if paralysed; she never knew how she got outside the house again. At the door she dropped on to a bench; her feet would carry her no further. She tried to reassure herself: most likely, restless as he was, he had gone out after some night game—what could he do to Joseph, quietly asleep somewhere—she shivered—on a soft pillow? And by day when everyone was up and about, nobody could touch or harm him.

It was her evil conscience that pursued her with these terrors, and she hid her face in her hands. "Wally, Wally, what art thou become?" Shamed, scorned, degraded in the eyes of men, and a sinner in the eyes of God. Where was water enough to purify her? Down below, there rushed the torrent— that—yes, that would clear her from every stain; if she threw herself into that cold flood, all would be washed away, her sorrow and her guilt—the whole unblest existence created only to horror and to strife at once done away with—annihilated. Yes, that were redemption—why did she hesitate? Away with the useless shell that held the soul in fetters of guilt and suffering! She started up, but she could not move, she fell back upon the bench. Was this down-trodden, deadened spirit still held to life then by some invisible thread?

There, God be praised! a footstep on the grass.

There came Vincenz. Now she could speak with him; all might yet be well.

"Saints above us!" exclaimed Vincenz, as she went forward to meet him, "is it thou?" He gazed at her as if she were a spirit. Wally saw in the morning twilight that he was pale and disturbed. His gun was on his shoulder.

"Vincenz," she said in a low voice, "hast thou shot anything?"

"Aye."

"What?" She looked at his game-bag, it was empty.

"Noble game," he whispered.

Wally shivered. "Where is it?"

"He lies in the Ache!"

Wally seized him by the arm, in her eyes was a gleam of frenzy. "Who?" she said.

"Dost need to ask?"

"Joseph!" she cried, and staggered back against the wall.

"It was a hard job," said Vincenz, wiping his brow; "I never thought he'd have come so soon within shot. The devil knows what brought him out and about by night. I thought I'd get up early, so as to be down in Sölden before he was stirring, and at the first step he walks right into my hands. But it was still so dark that the first shot missed, and the second only grazed him, but he must have turned giddy, for he stumbled on the bridge, and held on by the railing. I made the best of the chance,—I sprang behind him and pushed him over the rail."

A groan like a death-rattle burst from Wally, and as a vulture swoops upon his prey, she flew at Vincenz and seized his throat with both hands. "Thou liest, Vincenz, thou liest—it is not true, it cannot be—say it is not true, or I'll murder thee."

"On my soul, it's true;—didst suppose Vincenz 'd think twice when there was ought to do for thee?"

"Oh murder! most cruel and dastardly murder," sobbed Wally, trembling from head to foot, "so underhand, so cowardly, so base — that I never meant; in fair fight I meant that he should die. Cursed be thou in time and in eternity!—outcast and accursed now and hereafter. What can I do to thee? With tooth and nail thou ought to be torn in pieces."

"So these are the thanks I get?" said Vincenz between his teeth. "Did not thou bid me do it?"

"And if I did—what then? Was that a reason?" cried Wally wildly, "often one says in anger what afterwards one rues in bitterness. Could thou not wait till I had come to myself again after the awful shock? Joseph, Joseph!—wild and wicked I may be, but no murderess. Oh, why could thou not wait, only a few hours? Thy own wickedness it was that drove thee on, and thou could never rest till thou had worked it out."

"That's right, lay it all on me," growled Vincenz; "and yet thou's thy share in the mischief too."

"Aye," said Wally, "I have—and with thee I'll atone for it. For us two no mercy remains. Blood cries for blood—" She ground her teeth, and seizing Vincenz by the collar, dragged him forward with her.

"Wally, leave go of me!—what dost thou want? My God, are these the thanks I get? Mercy — Wally, thou'rt choking me—where art thou dragging me to?"

"To where we two belong," was the gloomy answer, and on she went as though borne by a whirlwind, up the ascent, on to the bridge where the sheer precipice overhangs the torrent—where the deed was done. "Down," was the one fearful word she thundered in his ear, "we two—together."

"God above us!" shrieked Vincenz in terror,

"thou swore that if I did the deed thou'd be my wife, and now wilt thou murder me?"

Wally laughed her fearful laugh of scorn. "Thou fool, when I fling myself down yonder with thee, shall not we two be together to all eternity? will thou try to save thy wolfish life?" And with the strength of a giant she grasped him in her arms, and hurried him forward to the low parapet that she might throw herself with him into the twilight gloom of the abyss.

"Help!" shrieked Vincenz involuntarily, and—

"Help!" sounded feebly, ghostly, like an echo from the depths.

Wally stood as if turned to stone and let go her hold of Vincenz. What was that? Some mocking goblin? "Did thou hear it?" she said to Vincenz.

"It was the echo," he said, and his teeth chattered.

"Hark—again!"

"Help!" sounded once more like a passing breath from the abyss.

"All good spirits be praised, it is he—he lives —he is clinging somewhere—he calls for help! Yes—I am coming, Joseph, only wait, Joseph—I am coming!" she shouted out with a voice like a trumpet into the depths, and with a voice like a trumpet-call she hailed the sleeping village as she flew along the street, knocking at every door. "Help, help—a man is perishing, save him—help, for God's sake, help—it's life or death!" And at the cry everyone sprang from his bed, and threw open the windows.

"What is it? what's the matter?"

"It's Joseph Hagenbach—he's fallen into the ravine," cried Wally, "ropes—bring ropes—only come quick—it may already be too late—it may perhaps be too late by the time we get there."

She flew like the wind, home to the farm, into the barn, collected all the ropes that were there, and knotted them together with trembling hands; but all she could tie together, ropes and lines and cords, were still not enough to reach into the depths where he lay—God only knew where.

Meanwhile the men came running together half-incredulous, half-amazed at the terrible news, and brought with them ropes, and hooks and lanterns —for it seemed as if to-day it would never be light—and there was questioning and advising and helpless bewilderment, for in the memory of man no one had ever fallen over the cliff, and here on the broad Plateau they were not provided with ready means of rescue as they are in places where the dizzy precipices and yawning clefts and chasms every year demand their victims. Thus they came at last to the spot, and a chill terror seized even the most cold-blooded as they bent over the railing, and looked down into the mysterious depths of the abyss in which nothing could be seen but the surging mists that rose up from the water. Vincenz had disappeared; all was solitary and silent as death far and wide, above and below. Wally gave a halloo so shrill that the air trembled; all listened with suspended breath—no answer.

"Joseph — where art thou?" she cried once more with a voice in whose tone the anguish of all suffering and desperate humanity seemed concentrated. All was still.

"He doesn't answer — he is dead!" sobbed Wally, and threw herself in despair upon the earth. "Now all is over!"

"Perhaps he's lost his senses, or is too weak to answer," said old Klettenmaier consolingly, then whispered in her ear. "Mistress, think of all the people."

She raised herself and pushed her disordered hair off her forehead. "Tie the ropes together; don't stand there doing nothing — what are you waiting for?" The men looked at her doubtingly. "We must at least try if he's not to be found," said Klettenmaier.

The men shook their heads, but began to fasten the cords together. "Who will let himself down by the rope?" they said.

"Who?" said Wally. Her black eyes flashed out of her pale face. "I will!" she said.

"Thou, Wally—thou's out of thy senses—the rope will scarce bear one, much less two."

"It need bear only one," said Wally gloomily, and seized the rope that it might be done quicker.

"It's impossible, Wally—thou'll have to tie thyself and him to it to come up again," said the men, dropping their arms helplessly; "the only thing to do is to send into the villages, and collect more ropes—"

"And meanwhile he'll fall to the bottom if he's lost his senses, and all will be too late," cried Wally desperately. "I'll not wait till more comes —give it me here—unwind the rope, and see how long it is—go on—unwind!" She shook out the coils of rope, and tried its length and strength; involuntarily the men took hold of it again, they unwound the huge coil, the preparations began to take shape and order. The men stepped out to make a chain. "It may reach far enough, but it'll never bear two."

"If it won't bear two, I'll send him up alone.

Where he has room to lie, I shall have room to stand. As soon as I've found a footing, I'll untie myself, and tie the rope round him; then draw him up, and I can wait till the rope comes down again—"

"Nay—that won't do—if he's weak or senseless he can't be pulled up alone; he'll be dashed and crushed against the cliff if there's no one with him to hold him off."

Wally stood as if thunderstruck—she had not thought of that. Again, then, she was thwarted— she was not to reach him, except down yonder, perhaps, in the cold bed of the Ache! The rope would not bear two, that she herself could see. "In the name of God," she said at last, and in spite of the fever that shook her, she stood there dignified and commanding in her firm resolve. She tied the rope round her waist, and took her Alpenstock in her hand. "Let me down, that I may at least seek him. If I find him, I'll stay with him and support him till you've brought another rope, and let it down to us. I'll wait patiently down there, even if I've to wait for hours hanging between earth and heaven till the other rope can come."

Old Klettenmaier fell on his knees before her. "Wally, Wally, don't thou do it, they all say the rope isn't safe. If it must be done, let me go—what does my old life matter? If I can do no good, at least thou'll see if the rope holds, and if it breaks, it'll only be me that's killed—not thee."

"Aye, Wally, hear him," said another, "he's in the right; don't thou go. Only wait, bethink thyself a little till help comes from the villages."

Wally threw up her arms, so that they all fell back. "When I was but a child, I did not wait to think before I took the vulture from its nest down the precipice—and shall I wait NOW when I go to seek Joseph? Speak no more to me—I will, I must go to him. Now—step back, unwind, hold fast!" And even as she spoke, she had sprung over the railing, whilst the men who formed the chain had to hold back with all their might, so great was the strain upon the rope.

"God Almighty help us," said Klettenmaier crossing himself, then ran off, as if Wally's words had reminded him of something. All gazed after her with horror as she slowly sank lower and lower into the sea of mist till it had swallowed her up and closed over her, never perhaps to be seen again. All stood speechless round the spot where she had disappeared, as round a grave; the tightly-strained rope alone gave intelligence of the movements of the death-defying diver in this sea of clouds, and on it every eye was fixed—would it break?—would it bear? And each time one of the hastily-tied knots was paid out, every heart beat louder—"Would it hold?"

The beads of sweat fell from the brows of the men who formed the chain, and involuntarily each tried once more the knots on which a human life depended. So passed minute after minute, heavy as lead,—as if time also were bound to some rope that dark powers refused to let go. Still the rope strained and swayed, still she must be hanging to it; she had not yet found a footing.

"It's coming to an end," cried the last man of the chain, "it's not long enough."

"God help us!" they all cried together, "not long enough!"

Only a few yards remained, and still no sign from below that Wally's end was attained. The men pressed together as close as they could to the edge of the precipice, paying out as much of the rope as they dared. If it were not long enough;— if all had been in vain;—if they should be obliged to draw up the hapless Wally, to set forth once more on the way of death!

There—there, the rope is suddenly loosened—it is slack—a fearful moment! Has it given way, or has its burden touched the ground?

The women pray aloud, the children cry. The

men begin slowly to pull in, but only a little way—
the rope is tight again. It is not broken, Wally has
found a footing, and now, listen! An echoing cry
rises from the depths, and a quivering response
bursts from every throat. Again the rope is slack,
they wind it in, and again it is loosened once or twice;
it would seem that Wally is climbing up the precipice. Meanwhile the day has broken, but a fine,
cold rain is drizzling down and the swirl of fog
below is thicker than ever. Now the rope sharply
jerked to the right takes a slanting direction; the
men follow it and pass from the left to the right
side of the bridge. Wally seems to mount higher
and higher; they continue to haul in.

"God be praised!" said some, "he cannot have
fallen so deep; if he lies so far up, he may still
live." "Perhaps she's only looking for him," said
others. Now another pull at the rope, and then a
sudden slackening, and a soul-piercing scream.

"It's broken!" shrieked the people.

No, it is taut again—perhaps it was a scream
of joy—perhaps she has found him. The women
fall on their knees, even the men pray, for though
all hated the haughty "peasant-mistress"—still, for
the devoted girl who hangs down there in the
chaos between life and death, every one that has a
human heart trembles. If only a ray of sunshine

would pierce the gloom for one single moment! All stand looking down, but they can distinguish nothing; they must leave it to time that passes with such slow reluctance, to reveal the event.

The rope remains immovable, but not another sound reaches them from below. Is it broken and caught on some point of rock, while Wally lies dashed to pieces below? Why is there no signal, no call? And hours must pass before they can get help from the villages round.

No one dares to speak a word—all stand listening with suspended breath. Suddenly old Klettenmaier comes running up, beckoning and shouting.

"See what I've got," he called out, showing a whole length of stout rope thrown over his shoulders. "Thank God, when Wally spoke of the vulture, it all at once struck me that old Luckard had had the rope laid by that Stromminger let Wally down to the vulture's nest with;—and there sure enough I found it, in the loft under a heap of old lumber."

"That is a find!" "Klettenmaier, that's a real godsend," cried the people confusedly. "God grant it may yet be of use," said the patriarch of the village, looking despondingly at the cord of deliverance, "she gives no farther sign!"

"The rope is pulled!" shouted the foremost
man of the chain, and at the same moment a cry
came up, so close at hand, that when all was
silent they could catch the words: "Is there no
more rope?"

"Ay, ay, plenty!" resounded joyfully from every
side. A grappling iron was fastened for an anchor
on to the end of the rope, a fresh chain of men
was formed, and it was cast into the impenetrably
shrouded abyss. The oldest of the peasants gave
the word of command—for the ropes must be paid
out exactly together, so that Wally might be close
to the injured man and support him. Not half so
far down as Wally had gone at first, the rope was
caught below, and held fast.

"Let out!" said the leader, in order that Wally
might have a few more yards to fasten round Joseph. "Enough," he called out then, and like
soldiers at the word of command, the men stood
awaiting the next order. Again a few minutes'
pause; she must make the loop securely and carefully, so that the senseless man, now so nearly
saved, might not fall again into the abyss.

"Tie it fast, Wally," panted Klettenmaier, half
beside himself.

"Yes, for God's sake, let her make it fast,"
echoed the people.

A thrice-repeated pull at both ropes at once. "Haul in!" commanded the leader, and his voice trembled as he spoke. The men at both ropes set their feet firmly in the ground, the veins swell in legs and arms and brows, sinewy hands are stretched forward to pull, and the lifting of the heavy loads begins. A fearful and responsible task!—if one fails, all is lost.

"Steady," warns the leader, "watch each other."

It is a solemn moment. Even the children dare not stir; nothing is audible far or near but the deep breath of the toiling men.

Now!—now they appear through the mist, more and more distinctly.—Wally emerges with one arm supporting the lifeless body that hangs to the saving rope, whilst with the other she powerfully bears off from the precipice with her Alpenstock, to keep herself and him from being dashed against it. In this way, as if rowing, she ascends upwards through the sea of clouds. And at last they are there, close to the edge,—one pull more, and they can be lifted up.

"Steady," says the leader—every breath is held —the last moment is the worst—if the rope were to break now!

But no, the foremost of the chain stoop and

seize them with a firm grasp, those behind hold fast to the rope.

"Up!" cry the men in front. They are raised —they are there—they are on firm ground, and a ringing shout of joy relieves the long-oppressed hearts of the bystanders. Wally has sunk speechless on the inanimate body of Joseph. She does not see, she does not hear, how all crowd round her and praise her—she lies with her face upon his breast—her strength is gone.

———

CHAPTER XIII.

Back to her Father.

In Wally's room, on Wally's bed, lay Joseph, stretched out, insensible. All was silent and still around him; she had sent every one away, she knelt by the bed, she hid her face in her convulsively clasped hands, and prayed.

"Oh, Lord God!—my God! my God! have mercy and let him live; take from me everything—everything—but let him live. I'll ask no more of him, I'll shun him—I'll leave him to Afra even—only he must not die!" And then she stood up again and made fresh bandages for his head where the blood flowed from a gaping wound, and for his breast that had been torn by the crag, and threw herself upon him as though with her body she would close those portals through which his life was streaming away.

"Oh, thou poor lad! thou poor lad! so stricken and brought down—oh, the sin of it—the sin of it! Wally, Wally, what hast thou done? Should thou not sooner have struck a knife into thine own heart—sooner have stood by at Afra's wedding, then gone home quietly and died, than have laid him there to see him perish like cattle that the butcher has felled?"

Thus she lamented out loud whilst she bound his wounds, turning against herself with the same anger with which she had been used to revenge herself on others. She would have torn her heart out with her own hands if she could, in the wild and frenzied remorse that had seized her. Just then the door opened softly. Wally looked round in astonishment, for she had forbidden any one to disturb her. It was the curé of Heiligkreuz. Wally stood before him as before her judge, pale, trembling in her very soul.

"God be praised!" cried the old man, "he is here then." He went up to the bed, looked at Joseph, and felt him. "Poor fellow," he said, "you have been roughly handled."

Wally set her teeth to keep herself from crying out at these words.

"How did they get him up again?" asked the priest, but Wally could not answer.

"Well, thank God, He has averted the worst in His mercy," continued the curé. "Perhaps he will get well, and you will then at least have no murder on your conscience, though before the eternal judge the intention is as bad as the deed."

Wally tried to speak.

"I know everything," he said with severity; "Vincenz came to me when he fled, and confessed all—your love and his jealousy. I refused him absolution, and sent him to join the Papal army; there he may earn God's forgiveness by good service to the Holy Father, or expiate his crimes by death. But what shall I say to thee, Wally?" He looked at her sadly and piercingly with his shrewd eyes.

Wally clasped her hands before her face. "Oh!" she cried aloud, "none can punish me with so bitter a punishment as I have brought on myself. There he lies dying, whom I loved best in all the world, and I have to tell myself that I did it. Can there be greater misery than that? Needs there anything more?"

The priest nodded his head. "This then is what you have done—you have become a rough piece of wood, fit to slay men with! It has happened as I told you; you have resisted the knife of God, and now the Lord casts you on one side and leaves the hard wood to burn in the fire of repentance."

"Ay, your reverence, it is so, but I know of water that will quench that fire. Into the Ache I will fling myself if Joseph dies—then all will be at an end."

"Alas, poor fool! do you think that is a flame that earthly water can quench? Do you really think that, with your earthly body, you can drown your immortal soul? That would burn in the tormenting flame of eternal remorse, even if all the seas in the world were poured upon it."

"What shall I do then?" said Wally gloomily; "what can I do but die?"

"Live and suffer: that is nobler than death."

Wally shook her head. Her dark eyes looked vaguely before her. "I cannot—I feel it—I cannot live, the phantom maidens thrust me down—all has happened as they threatened me in my dream: there lies Joseph crushed and broken, and I must follow him; it is fated so, and it must happen so, none can prevent it."

"Wally, Wally!" cried the priest, clasping his hands in horror, "what are you saying? The phantom maidens? What phantom maidens? In Heaven's name! do we live in the dark heathen times when men believed that evil spirits made sport of them? I will tell you who the phantom maidens are:—your own passions. If you had learnt to tame your own wild unbridled will, Joseph would never have fallen over the precipice. It is easy to lay the blame of your own evil deeds to the influence of hostile powers. For that it is that our Lord came to us, to teach us to acknowledge that we bear the evil in ourselves, and must fight with it. If we control ourselves, we control the mysterious powers which drove even the giants of the past to destruction, because with all their strength they had no moral power to withstand them. And with all your strength, your hardness and your daring, you are but a pitiful, weak creature, so long as you do not know what every homely, simple handmaid of the Lord performs, who, every day in the strict discipline of her cloister-life, lays on God's altar the dearest wish of her heart, and esteems herself blessed in the sacrifice! If you had only one glimmer of such greatness in your soul, you need have no more fear of the 'phantom maidens,' and your foolish dreams would no longer direct your destiny, but your own clear and conscious will. Reflect for once whether that were not nobler and happier."

Wally leaned against the bed-post; she felt as if raised to a newly-awakened and noble consciousness. "Yes," she said shortly and decidedly, and crossed her arms on her heaving breast, "your reverence is right—I understand, and I will try."

"I will try!" repeated the old priest, "once before you said that to me—but you did not keep your word."

"This time, your reverence, I will keep it," said Wally, and the priest silently admired the expression with which she spoke the simple words.

"What security will you give me?" he said.

Wally laid her hand on Joseph's wounded breast, and two large tears sprang to her eyes; no spoken vow could have said more. The wise priest was silent also, he knew no more was needed.

The wounded man turned in his bed and muttered some unintelligible words. Wally made him a fresh bandage for his head; he half-opened his eyes, but closed them again and fell back in a death-like slumber.

"If only the doctor would come!" said Wally, seating herself on a stool by the bed. "What o'clock may it be?"

The priest looked at his watch. "What time did you send for him?" he said.

"About five o'clock."

"Then he cannot be here yet. It is only ten o'clock, and it is quite three hours to Sölden."

"Only ten o'clock," Wally repeated in a low voice, and the good priest was filled with pity to see her sit there so quietly, her hands folded in her lap, whilst her heart beat with anguish so that it could be heard.

He bent over the sick man, and felt his head

and his hands, "I think you may be easy, Wally,"
he said, "he does not appear to me like a dying
man."

Wally sat motionless, gazing fixedly before her.
"If the doctor comes and says that he'll live, I care
for nothing more in this world," she said.

"That is right, Wally, I am glad to hear you
say that," said the curé approvingly, "and now re-
late to me how it was that Joseph was saved—that
will help to shorten the time till the doctor comes."

"There's not much to tell," answered Wally
shortly.

"Nay, it is a noble deed that does honour to
the men of the Sonnenplatte," said the priest, "were
you not there?"

"Oh yes!"

"Well then, be less short in your answers. I
spoke with no one on the way, and have heard nothing about it. Who fetched him up from the ravine?"

"I!"

"God be gracious! You, Wally? you yourself?"
cried the old man, staring at her with astonishment.

"Yes—I!"

"But how can you have done it?"

"They let me down by a rope, and I found
him fixed between a rock and the trunk of a fir-
tree; if the tree had not been there he must have

fallen into the torrent, and no one'd ever have seen him alive again."

"Child," cried the old man, "that is a great thing to have done."

"May be so," she answered quietly, almost hardly, "as I'd had him thrown yonder, it was for me to fetch him up again."

"You are right,—that was only fair," said the priest, controlling his emotion with difficulty. "But it is not the less an act of atonement that may take some part of the guilt from your hapless soul."

"That is all nothing," said Wally, shaking her head. "If he dies, it's I that have murdered him."

"That is true, but you gave a life for a life. You risked your own to save his; you have atoned as far as was in your power for the crime you have committed—the issue is in God's hands."

Wally heaved a deep sigh; she could not take in the comfort that lay in the priest's words. "The issue is in God's hand," she repeated out of the depths of her burdened heart.

The eye of the priest rested on her with content; God would not reject this soul, in spite of its great faults and imperfections. Never yet, old as he was, had he met with her equal in power for good, as for evil. He looked at the wounded man who unconsciously clenched his fist in defiance. It almost angered him that he should despise the noblest gift that earth can offer man—a devoted love; that through his indifference he should have had it in his power to harden a heart so noble in its nature and capable of such high-minded sacrifice. "You stupid peasant-lout," he muttered between his teeth.

Wally looked at him enquiringly: she had not understood.

There was a knock at the door, and at the same moment the doctor entered the room. Wally trembled so that she was obliged to hold by the bedpost. Here was the man on whose lips hung redemption or condemnation. A crowd of people pressed in after him to hear what he would say, but he soon turned them all out again. "This is no place for curiosity; the sick man must have the most perfect quiet," he said decidedly, and shut the door. He was a man of few words. Only, when he took the bandage from the sick man's head, "There has been foul play again here," he muttered.

Wally stood white and silent as a statue. The curé purposely avoided looking at her; he feared to disturb her self-possession. The examination began; anxious silence reigned in the little chamber. Wally stood by the window with averted face while the surgeon examined the wounds and used his probe. She had picked up something from the ground which she held convulsively clasped between her hands, and pressed again and again to her lips. It was the thorn-crowned head of the Redeemer that she had broken in the night. "Forgive, forgive," she prayed, pale and quivering in her deadly anguish. "Have mercy on me—I deserve nothing—but let Thy mercy be greater than my sin."

"None of the wounds are mortal," said the doctor in his dry way. "The fellow must have joints like an elephant."

Then Wally's strength went from her. The chord, too long and too highly strung, gave way, and loudly sobbing she threw herself on her knees by the bed, and buried her face in Joseph's pillows. "Oh, thank God! Thank God!"

"What is the matter with her?" asked the doctor. The priest answered him by a sign that he understood.

"Come, collect yourself," he said, "and help me to put on the bandages."

Wally sprang up at once, wiped the tears from her eyes, and lent a helping hand. The priest observed with secret pleasure that she assisted the doctor as carefully and skilfully as a sister of charity; she did not tremble, she wept no more, she showed a steady and quiet self-control—the true self-control of love. And withal there was a glory on her brow, a glory in the midst of sorrow, so that the priest hardly knew her.

"She will do yet—she will do," he said joyfully to himself, like a gardener who sees some treasured faded plant suddenly put forth new shoots.

When the bandages were all fixed and the doctor had given his further orders, the priest went out with him, and Wally remained alone with Joseph. She sat down on the stool by the bed and rested her arms on her knees. He breathed softly and regularly now, his hand lay close to her on the counterpane—she could have kissed it without moving from her place. But she did not do it, she felt as if now she dared not touch even one of his fingers. If he had lain there dying or dead, then she would have covered him with kisses, as heretofore, when she believed him lost; the dead would have belonged to her—on the living she had no claim! He had died to her in the moment when the doctor had said he would live, and she buried him with anguish as for the dead in her heart, while the message of his resurrection came to her as the message of redemption. So she sat long, motionless by the side of the bed with her

eyes fixed on Joseph's beautiful, pale face—suffering
to the utmost what a human soul can suffer—but
suffering patiently. She neither sighed nor lamented
now, nor clenched her fist as formerly, in anger at
her own pain; she had in this hour learnt the
hardest of all lessons — she had learnt to endure.
What sort of right had she, the guilty one, to complain—what better did she deserve? How could
she dare still to wish for him, she who had almost
been his murderess? How could she dare even to
raise her eyes to him? No, she would bewail herself no more. "Thou dear God, let me expiate it
as Thou will—no punishment is too great for such
as I am—" So she prayed, and bowed her head
humbly on her clasped hands.

All at once the door was flung open, and with
a cry of "Joseph, my own Joseph!" a girl rushed
in, past Wally, and threw herself weeping upon
Joseph; it was Afra. Wally had started up as if a
snake had touched her: for an instant the battle
raged within, the last and hardest fight. She grasped
herself, as it were, with her own arms, as though
to keep herself back from falling upon the girl and
tearing her away from the bed—from Joseph. So
she stood for a time, while Afra sobbed violently
on Joseph's breast; then her arms fell by her side
as if paralyzed, and beads of cold sweat stood on

her brow. What would she have? Afra was in her rights.

"Afra," she said in a low voice, "if thou truly loves Joseph, be still and cease these cries—the doctor says he must have perfect quiet."

"Who can be still that has a heart, and sees the lad lie there like that?" lamented Afra, "it's easy for thee to talk, thou doesn't love him as I do. Joseph is all I have—if Joseph dies I am all alone in the world! Oh Joseph, dear Joseph—wake up, look at me—only once—only one word!" and she shook him in her arms.

A low groan escaped from Joseph's lips and he murmured a few unintelligible words.

Then Wally stepped forward and took Afra gently but firmly by the arm; not a muscle of her pale face moved.

"I have this to say to thee, Afra: Joseph is here under my protection, and I am responsible for all being done according to the doctor's orders; and this is my house that thou'rt in, and if thou will not do what I tell thee, and leave Joseph in peace, as the doctor wishes, I'll use my right and put thee out at the door, till thou's come to thy senses and art fit to take care of him again—then," her voice trembled, "I'll leave him to thee."

"Oh, thou wicked thing, thou—" cried Afra

passionately, "thou'd turn me out of the house because I weep for Joseph? Dost think everyone has so hard a heart as thou, and can stand there looking on like a stone? Let go my arm! I've a better right than thou to Joseph, and if thou doesn't like to hear me cry, I'll take him up in my arms and carry him home—there at least I can weep as much as I please. I'm only a poor servant-maid, but if I'd to pay for it by serving all my days for nothing, I'd sooner nurse him in my own little room than let myself be shown the door by thee—thou haughty peasant-mistress!"

Wally let go of Afra's arm; she stood before her with a white face, and with marks of such deadly suffering round her closed lips, that Afra cast down her eyes in shame, as if she divined how unjust she had been.

"Afra," said Wally, "thou's no need to show such hatred, I don't deserve it of thee; for it was for thee I fetched him out of the abyss—not for me,—and it is for thee he will live, not for me! Look here, Afra, only an hour ago I'd sooner have throttled thee than have left thee by his bedside—but now all is broken, my spirit, and my pride, and—my heart," she added low to herself. "And so I'll make way for thee willingly, for he loves thee, and with me he'll have nought to do. Stay

thou with him in peace—thou need not take away
the poor sick man. Sooner will I go myself. You
two can stay at the farm so long as you will—I
will account for it with him to whom it belongs
now. And I will take care of you in everything,
for you are both of you poor, and cannot marry if
you have nothing. And so perhaps some day
Joseph will bless the Vulture-maiden—"

"Wally, Wally," cried Afra. "What art thou
thinking of? I pray thee—oh Joseph, Joseph—if
only I might speak!"

"Let it be," said Wally, "keep thyself quiet—
for love of Joseph, keep thyself quiet. And now
let me go in peace; torment me no more, for go I
must. Only one thing I pray thee in return for
what I've done for thee, take good care of him.
Promise me thou will, that I may go with an easy
mind."

"Wally," said Afra entreatingly, "don't thou do
that, don't go away! What will Joseph say when
he hears we've driven thee out of thy own house?"

"Spare all words, Afra," said Wally firmly,
"when once I have said a thing, it stands, come
what máy."

She went to the chest, and took out a change
of clothes, which she tied together in a bundle and
threw over her shoulder. Then from a box she

took a bundle of linen. "See, Afra," she said, "here is old and fine linen that thou'll need for bandages, and here is coarser to make lint, which the doctor will want when he comes this evening. Look, there are scissors—thou must cut it into strips the length of my finger. Dost understand? And every quarter of an hour, thou must put a fresh bandage on his head to draw the heat out. Tell me, can I trust thee not to forget? Think what it would be if, after I have fetched him out of the ravine, I should find that thou—thou had been careless in nursing him—here, at his bedside. And see, he must always lie with his head high, that the blood may not go to it—and shake the pillows up often. That is all, I think, now—I know of nought else. Ah, my God, thou'll not be able to lift him and lay him down as I do—thou hasn't got the strength. Get Klettenmaier to help thee; he is trustworthy. Now I leave him in thy hands—" Her voice failed her, her knees trembled, she could hardly hold the bundle that she carried. She threw a last glance at the wounded man: "God keep thee!" she said, and left the room.

Outside, the priest was talking with Klettenmaier. Wally went up to them.

"Klettenmaier," she shouted in the old man's ear, "Go in and help Afra to mind Joseph; Afra is there now in my place. Joseph will stay at the farm, and I am going away. You are all to treat Joseph as if he were the master, and to obey him as if I were by, till I come back; and woe to you, if he has to complain of ought. Let all the servants know!"

Klettenmaier had understood, and shook his head, but he did not venture to make any remark. "Good-bye, mistress," he said, "Come back again soon."

"Never!" said Wally softly.

Klettenmaier went into the house; Wally stood before the priest, and met his questioning glance. "Now nought is my own that my heart clings to, but the vulture," she said sadly, as if exhausted. "But him I cannot give up—he must come with me. Come, Hansl." She beckoned to the bird, which sat puffed up and drowsy on a railing; he came flying towards her with difficulty.

"Thou must learn to fly again now, Hansl," she said, "we're going away."

"Wally," said the priest, much concerned, "what do you mean to do?"

"Your reverence, I must go away—Afra is in there! Is it not plain that I cannot stay? I will do anything, I will all my life go bare and home-less, and wander through the country, and leave everything to him—everything—but I cannot look on at his Afra's love—only that I cannot—cannot bear!" She set her teeth to keep back the springing tears.

"And for his sake you will really give up house and home? Do you know what you are doing, my child?"

"The farm no longer belongs to me, your reverence. Since yesterday I've known that it belongs to Vincenz, whenever he puts in his claim. But my money, what I have besides, shall be for Joseph. If he is crippled by my fault, and cannot earn his bread,—it is my accursed guilt, and I must provide for him."

"What, is it possible," cried the priest, "that your father disinherited you of house and home?"

"What do I care for house and home? The home I belong to is always ready," said Wally.

"Child," said the old man, much disturbed, "you would not do yourself an injury?"

"No, your reverence, never now. I see now how right you are in everything, and that God Almighty will not be defied by us. Perhaps, when He sees that I truly repent, He'll have pity on me and grant peace to my weary soul."

"Now blessed be the hour, hard though it may have been, that broke your proud spirit! Now

Wally, you are truly great! But where are you going, my child? Will you go to some charitable refuge? Shall I take you to the Carmelites?"

"No, your reverence, that would never suit the Vulture-maiden. I cannot be shut up in a cell between walls — under God's free sky, as I have lived, will I die—I should feel as if God could not come through such thick walls. I'll repent and pray as if I were in a church, but I must have the rocks and the clouds about me, and the wind whistling in my ears, or I couldn't get on at all— you understand, do you not?"

"Yes, I understand, and it would be folly to try to dissuade you. But where then are you going?"

"I'm going back to my father Murzoll—there is now my only home."

"Do as you will," said the priest. "Go in God's name, my child—I can part from you in peace, for wherever you go now—it is back to your Father!"

———

CHAPTER XIV.

The Message of Grace.

HIGH up on the lonely Ferner, near her stony father, once more sits the outcast, solitary child of man—spell-bound, as it were, like a part of the dizzy heights from which she looks down on the little world below, in which no space could be found for the large and alien heart that had matured in the wilderness among the glacier-storms. Men have hunted and driven her forth, and that has been fulfilled that her dream foretold, the mountain has adopted her as its child. She belongs to the mountain now; stone and ice are her home—and yet she cannot turn to stone herself, and the warm and hapless human heart is silently bleeding to death up here between stone and ice.

Twice had the moon's disk waxed and waned since the day when Wally sought this, her last refuge. No familiar face from amongst the dwellers in the valley had she seen. Only once the priest had dragged his old' and frail body up the mountain to tell her that Joseph was recovering; further, that news had come from Italy that shortly after enlisting Vincenz had been shot, and had left to her the whole of his possessions. Then she had folded her hands on her knees, and said quietly, "It is well for him—it is soon over," as if she envied him.

"But what will you do with all this money?" the priest had asked her, "who will manage your immense property? You must not let it all go to ruin."

"Gold and goods plentiful as straw—and no help in them," said Wally, "they cannot buy for me one short hour of happiness. When time has gone by, and I can think of things again, I'll go down to Imst and make it all sure that my property becomes Joseph's. For myself I'll keep only enough to have a little house built further on, under the mountain, for the winter—but now I must have peace, I can care for nothing now. Manage things for me, your reverence, and see that the servants get their due, and give the poor what they need; there shall be no poor on the Sonnenplatte from this day forward."

Thus briefly had she settled her worldly affairs as though on the brink of the next world: it remained to her only to await her hour—the hour of deliverance. It seemed to her as if God had said by the mouth of the priest, "Thou shalt not come to me, till I myself fetch thee." And now she waited till He should fetch her—but how long, how terribly long the time might be! She looked at her powerfully-built frame—it was not planned for an early death, and yet death was her only hope. She knew and understood that she must not end her days with violence, that her atonement must be consecrated; but she thought—surely she might *help* the good God to set her free when it should please Him! And so she did everything that might injure the strongest body. It was not suicide to take only just enough nourishment to keep herself from starving—fasting is ever a help to penitence—nor to expose herself day and night to the storm and rain from which even the vulture took shelter in a cleft of the rock, so that wet, frost, and privation began gradually to undermine her healthy constitution. It was not self-murder to climb the cliffs no mortal foot had trodden, it was only to give the good God the opportunity to fling her down—if He would! And with a sort of gloomy pleasure she watched her beautiful body waste away, she felt her strength diminish, often she sank down with fatigue if she had wandered far, and when she climbed, her knees trembled and her breath grew short. Thus she sat one day weary on one of Murzoll's highest peaks. Around her, piled one upon another, rose white pinnacles and blocks of ice; it looked like a church-yard in winter where the snow-covered grave-stones stand in rows side by side, no longer veiled by clinging leaf or blossom. Immediately at her feet lay the green-gleaming sea of ice with its frozen waves, that flowed onwards as far as the pass leading over the mountain. Deepest silence as of the tomb dwelt in this frozen, motionless upper world. The distance with its endless perspective of mountains lay dreamily veiled in soft noonday mists. On Si-milaun, close to the brown Riesenhorn, nestled a small, bright cloud, that clung to it caressingly and was wafted up to sink again, till at last, torn on the sharp edges of the frightful precipices, it disappeared.

Wally lay supported on her elbow, and her eye mechanically followed the drift of the tiny cloud. The mid-day sun burned above her head, the vulture sat not far off, lazily pruning himself and spreading his wings. Suddenly he became uneasy, turned his head as if listening, stretched his neck, and flew croaking a short way higher up. Wally raised herself a little to see what had startled the bird. There, over the slippery, fissured glacier came a human form straight towards the rock where Wally sat. She recognized the dark eyes, the short, black beard, she saw the friendly glance and greeting, she heard the "Jodel" that he sent up to her —as once years ago, when from the Sonnenplatte she had seen him pass through the gorge with the stranger—she, an innocent, hopeful child in those days, not yet cast out and cursed by her father— not yet an incendiary—not yet a murderess. As a whole landscape bursts from the darkness with all its heights and depths revealed, under a flash of lightning—so the whole destined chain of events passed before her soul, and shuddering, she recognized the depth to which she was fallen.

What had she been then—and what was she now? And what did he seek who had never sought her then, what did he seek now of her, the condemned one—the dead-alive?

She gazed downwards in unspeakable terror. "Oh God! he is coming," she cried aloud, and clung to the rock in mortal anguish as if it were the hand of her stony father. "Joseph—stay below —not up here—for God's sake not up here—go— turn back—I cannot, will not see thee—;" but Joseph, who had mounted the rock at a quick run, was coming towards her. Wally hid her face against the stone, stretching out her hands, as if to defend herself against him. "Can one be alone nowhere in this world?" she cried, trembling from head to foot. "Dost thou not hear? Leave me. With me thou'st nought to do—I am dead —as good as dead am I—can I not even die in peace?"

"Wally, Wally, art thou beside thyself?" cried Joseph, and he pulled her from the rock with his powerful arms, as one might loosen some close-growing moss. "Look at me, Wally—for God's sake—why will thou not look at me? I am Joseph, Joseph whose life thou saved—that's not a thing one does for those one cannot bear to look at."

He held her in his arms, she had fallen on one knee, she could not move, she could not defend herself; she was no longer the Wally of former days, she was weak and powerless. Like a victim beneath the sacrificial knife, she bowed her head as if to meet the last stroke.

"Good Heavens, maiden! thou looks ready to die. Is this the haughty Wallburga Stromminger? Wally, Wally—speak then—come to thyself. This comes of living up here in the wilds where one might forget to speak one's mother-tongue almost. Thou'rt quite fallen away; come, lean on me and I'll lead thee down to thy hut. I'm no hero myself yet, but even so I've somewhat more strength than thee. Come—one gets dizzy up here, and I've much to say to thee, Wally—much to say."

Almost without will of her own, Wally let herself be led step by step, as, without speaking, he guided her uncertain footsteps over the glacier and down to her hut. There however they found the herdsman, and pausing therefore, Joseph let the girl glide from his support on to a meadow of mountain grass. She sat silent and resigned with folded hands; it was God's will to send her this trial also, and she prayed only that she might remain steadfast.

Joseph placed himself beside her, rested his chin on his hand, and looked with glowing eyes into her grief-worn face.

"I have much to account for to thee, Wally," he said earnestly, "and I should have come long ago if the doctor and the curé would have let me; but they said it might cost me my life if I went up the mountain too soon, and I thought that were a pity—for—now I first rightly value my life, Wally—" he took her hand, "since thou'st saved it —for when I heard that, I knew how it stood with thee—and just so it stands with me, Wally!" He stroked her hand gently.

Wally snatched it from him in sheer terror; it almost took her breath away.

"Joseph, I know now what thou would say! Thou think'st that because I saved thy life, thou must love me out of gratitude and leave Afra in the lurch after all. Joseph, that thou need not think, for so sure as there is a God in Heaven— wretched am I and bad—but not so bad as to take a reward I don't deserve, nor to let a heart be given me like wages—a heart too that I must steal from another. Nay, that the Vulture-maiden will not do—whatever else she may have done! Thank God, there's still some wickedness even I am not capable of," she added softly to herself. And collecting all her strength, she stood up and would have gone to the hut where the herdsman sat whistling a tune. But Joseph held her fast in both arms.

"Wally, hear me first," he said.

"Nay, Joseph!" she said with white lips, but proudly erect, "not another word. I thank thee for thy good intention—but thou dostn't know me yet."

"Wally, I tell thee thou must hear me for a moment—dost understand? Thou *must.*" He laid his hand on her shoulder and fixed his eyes on her with an expression so imperious that she broke down and gave way.

"Speak then'," she said as if exhausted, and seated herself, far from him, on a stone.

"That is right—now I see thou can obey," he said, smiling good-humouredly.

He stretched his finely-formed limbs on the grass, laid the jacket he had thrown off under his elbow and supported himself on it; his warm breath floated towards Wally as he spoke. She sat motionless with downcast eyes; the internal struggle gradually brought the hot colour to her face, but outwardly she was calm, almost indifferent.

"See, Wally,—I will tell thee exactly how it is," Joseph went on, "I could never bear thee formerly, because I didn't know thee. I heard so much of how wild and rough thou wert, and so I took a bad opinion of thee and would never have to do with thee at all. That thou'rt a fine and handsome maid I could see all the while—but I didn't *want* to see! So I always kept out of thy way, till the quarrel happened between thee and Afra—but that I could not let pass. For see, Wally—what is done to Afra is done to me, and when Afra is hurt it cuts me to the heart, for thou must know—well, it must come out, my mother in her grave will forgive me—Afra is my sister."

Wally started back, and stared at him as if in a dream. He was silent for a moment, and wiped his forehead with his linen sleeve. "It's not right for me to talk about it," he continued, "but thou must know, and thou'll let it go no further. My mother told me on her deathbed that before ever she knew my father, she had a child out there in Vintschgau, and I solemnly promised her that I would care for the lass as a sister, and it's for that I fetched her from across the mountains and brought her to the Lamb so that she might be near me. But we two promised each other that we'd keep it secret and not bring shame on our mother in her grave. Now dost thou understand how I couldn't let an injury to my sister pass un-punished, and stood up for her when she was wronged?"

Wally sat like a statue and struggled for breath. She felt as if the mountains and the whole world were whirling round her. Now all was clear—now too she understood what Afra had said by Joseph's bedside. She held her head with both hands, as if she could not grasp the meaning of it all. If it were indeed true, how gigantic was the wrong she had done. It was not a heartless man who had

scorned her for a lowly maid-servant — it was a
brother fulfilling his duty to a sister that she
would have killed—she would have bereft a poor
orphan of her last remaining stay for the sake of a
blind movement of jealousy. "Good God, if it had
been so!" she said to herself. She felt giddy—she
buried her face in her hands, and a dull groan
escaped her. Joseph, who did not observe her
agitation, went on.

"So it came to pass that up at the Lamb I
swore before them all that I would take down thy
pride, and do to thee as thou'd done to Afra, and
so we hatched the plot among us, in spite of Afra
who'd not have had it done. And all went well; but
when we wrestled with one another, and when that
dear and beautiful bosom lay upon my heart, and
when I kissed thee, it was as if my veins were
filled with fire. I'd say no word to thee, because
I'd been thy enemy so long,—but from hour to
hour the fire grew, and in the night I clasped
my pillow to me and thought that it was thou,
and when I woke, I cried out loud for thee and
sprang out of bed for the ferment and fever I
was in."

"Stop, stop—thou'rt killing me," cried Wally,
with cheeks and brow aflame; but he went on passionately: "So I went out whilst it was still night,

and wandered up to the Sonnenplatte. I'll tell thee all,—I meant to knock at thy window before break of day, and I was full of joy to think how thou'd put out thy sleepy face, and how I'd hold thy head, and make amends for all, and ask thy pardon a thousand, thousand times. And then — then a shot whistled past my head, and directly after another hit my shoulder, and as I stumbled some one sprang on me from behind and hurled me down from the bridge. And I thought, now all is over with love and everything else. But thou came, thou angel in maiden's form, and took pity on me, and saved me, and cared for me—Oh, Wally!" He threw himself at her feet, "Wally, I cannot thank thee as I ought—but all the love of all the men in the world put together is not so great as the love I have for thee."

Then Wally's strength gave way altogether — with a heart-rending cry she thrust Joseph from her, and flung herself in wild despair face downwards on the earth. "Oh, so happy as I might have been—and now all is over—all, all!"

"Wally, for God's sake!—I believe thou'rt really mad! What is over? If thee and me love each other, all is well!"

"Oh Joseph, Joseph, thou doesn't know—nothing

can ever be between us two; oh, thou doesn't know, I am outcast and condemned — thy wife I can never be—trample on me, strike me dead—me it was that had thee flung down yonder."

Joseph shrank back at the awful words — he was not yet sure that Wally was not mad. He had sprung up, and was looking down at her in horror.

"Joseph," whispered Wally, and clasped his knees, "I've loved thee ever since I've known thee, and it was because of thee that my father sent me up to the Hochjoch, because of thee that I set fire to his house, because of thee that for three years I wandered lonely in the wilds, and was hungry and frozen and would have died sooner than be married to another man. And out of pure jealousy I treated Afra as I did, because I thought she was thy love and would take thee from me. And thou came at last after long, long years that I had waited for thee, and thou asked me to the dance like a bridegroom—and I believed it, my heart was bursting for joy, and I let thee kiss me as a bride, but thou — thou mocked me before everyone — *mocked* me!—for all the true love with which I had longed for thee—for all the sore trouble that I had borne for thee—then all at once everything was changed, and I bade Vincenz kill thee."

Joseph covered his face with his hands. "That is horrible," he said in an undertone.

"Then in the night I repented," Wally went on, "and I went out, and would have hindered it—but it was too late. And now thou'st come to tell me that thou loves me, and all would be well if I could stand before thee with a clear conscience. And I have brought it all on myself with my blind rage and wickedness. I thought no wrong could be so great as that thou did to me, and it is all nothing to what I have done to myself—but it serves me right—it serves me quite right."

There was a long silence. Wally had pressed her damp brow against Joseph's knee, her whole body shook as in a death-agony. An agonizing minute passed by. Then she felt a hand gently raise her face, and Joseph's large eyes looked down on her with a wonderful expression.

"Thou poor Wally!" he said softly.

"Joseph, Joseph, thou mustn't be so good to me," cried Wally trembling, "take thy gun and kill me dead—I'll hold still and never shrink, but bless thee for the deed."

He raised her from the ground, he took her in his arms, he laid her head on his breast and smoothed her disordered hair, then kissed her passionately. "And STILL I love thee!" he cried in a voice like a shout, so that the words rang back exultingly from the desert walls of ice.

Wally stood there hardly conscious, motionless, almost sinking under the flood of happiness that flowed over her. "Joseph, is it possible? Can thou really forgive me—can the great God forgive me?" she whispered breathlessly.

"Wally! He who could listen to thy words and look in thy wasted face, and could yet be hard to thee—that man would have a stone in the place of a heart. I'm a hard fellow, but I could not do that."

"Oh God!" said Wally, and the tears rushed to her eyes, "when I think that I would have stilled *that* heart for ever—!" She wrung her hands in despair: "Oh thou good lad—the better and the dearer thou art to me, so much the more terrible is my remorse. Oh, my peace is gone, for ever gone, in earth and in Heaven. Thy servant will I be, not thy wife—on thy door-step will I sleep, not at thy side—I'll serve thee, and work for thee, and do all thy will before thou can speak the word. And if thou strike me, I'll kiss thy hand, and if thou tread on me, I'll clasp thy knee—and beg and pray till thou'rt good to me again. And if thou grant me nought but the breath of thy lips, and a glance and a word—still I'll be content—it'll still be more than I deserve."

"And dost think that I should be content?" said Joseph hotly, "dost think a glance and a breath are enough for me? Dost think I'd suffer that thou should lie on the doorstep, and me inside? Dost think I would not open the door and fetch thee in? Dost think perhaps that thou would stay outside, when I called to thee to come?"

Wally tried to free herself from his grasp; she hid her glowing face in her clasped hands.

"Be at peace, sweet soul," Joseph went on in his deep, harmonious voice, and drew her towards him. "Be at peace, and take that which our Lord God sends thee — thou mayst, for thou hast atoned nobly. Torment thyself no more with self-reproach, for I also have sinned heavily towards thee, and provoked thee cruelly and rewarded thy long love and faith with mockery and scorn. No wonder that thy patience gave way at last—what else could one expect?—thou'rt only the Vulture Wally! But thou's quickly repented thee, and despised death itself to bring me from the depths where no man would have had the heart to go, and had me carried to thy room, and laid upon thy bed, and thyself hast tended me, till that foolish

Afra came and drove thee away, because thou thought she was my love. And thou wished to give us all thy property that I might be able to marry Afra — as thou thought! And then came away to the wilderness with thy heavy sorrow! Oh, thou poor soul, nought but heart-ache hast thou had for my sake since thou's known me, and shall I not love thee now and shall we know no happiness together? Nay, Wally, and if the whole world were hard to thee—it's all one to me, I take thee in my arms, and none shall do thee an injury."

"Is it really true that out of all my shame and misery thou'll take me to thy heart, thy great and noble heart? Thou'll have no fear of the wild Vulture-maiden that's done so many wicked things?"

"I fear the Vulture-maiden — I, Joseph the Bear-slayer? No, thou dear child, and were thou still wilder than thou art, I fear thee not, I'll conquer thee, that I told thee once before in hatred—I tell it thee now in love. And even if I could not tame thee, if I knew that within a fortnight thou'd murder me, I would not leave thee —I *could* not leave thee. A hundred times have I climbed after a chamois when I knew that each step might cost me my life—and yet would never leave it, and thou—art thou not worth far, more to me than any chamois? See Wally—for a single hour of thee as thou art to-day, to see thee look at me and cling to me as now, will I gladly die." He pressed her to him in a breathless embrace. "A fortnight hence thou'll be my wife, and have no thought of killing me—I *know* it, for now I know thy heart."

Then Wally sprang up, and raised her arms towards heaven. "Oh, Thou great and merciful God," she cried, "I will praise Thee and bless Thee my whole life long, for it is more than earthly happiness that Thou hast sent me—it is a message of Grace!"

It was now evening; a mild countenance looked down on them as in friendly greeting; the full moon stood above the mountain. On the valleys lay the shades of evening—it was too late now to descend the mountain-side. They went into the hut, kindled a fire and sat down on the hearth. It was an hour of sweet confidence after long years of silence. On the roof sat the Vulture and dreamed that he was building himself a nest, the rush of the night-wind round the hut was like the sound of harps, and through the little window shone a star.

Next morning Wally and Joseph stood at the door of the hut ready to set out homewards.

18*

"Farewell, God keep thee, Father Murzoll," said Wally, and the first gleam of morning showed a tear glittering in her eye, "I shall never come back to thee more. My happiness lies down yonder now, but yet I thank thee for giving me a home so long, when I was homeless. And thou, old hut, thou'll be empty now, but when I sit with my dearest husband down there in a warm room, I'll still think of thee, and how long nights through I've shivered and wept beneath thy roof, and will always be humble and thankful."

She turned and laid her hand on Joseph's arm. "Come, Joseph, that we may be at the good priest's at Heiligkreuz before mid-day."

"Aye, come—I'm taking thee home, my beautiful bride! You see, you phantom maidens, I've won her, and she belongs to me—in spite of you and all bad spirits."

And he threw out a "Jodel" into the blue distance, that sounded like a hymn of rejoicing on the day of resurrection.

"Be quiet," said Wally, laying her hand on his mouth in alarm, "thou mustn't defy them." But then she smiled with a serene look. "Ah no," she said, "there's no more 'phantom maidens' and no more bad spirits—there is only God."

She looked back once more. The snowy peaks of the Ferner glowed around in the morning light. "Still it is beautiful up here," she said with lingering footsteps.

"Art sorry to come down yonder with me?" asked Joseph.

"If thou wast to lead me into the deepest pit under the earth where no gleam of day ever shone, still I'd go with thee and never question nor complain," she said, and her voice sounded so wonderfully soft that Joseph's eyes were moist.

There was a sudden rush down from the roof of the hut. "Oh, my Hansl—I'd almost forgotten thee!" cried Wally. "And thou—?" she said smiling at Joseph, "thou must make friends with him, for now you two are brothers in fate. I fetched thee from the precipice as well as him."

So they went down the mountain side. It was a modest wedding procession, no splendour but the golden crown that the morning sunshine wove around the bride's head—no follower but the vulture that circled high in the air above them—but in their hearts was hardly-won, deeply-felt, unspeakable joy.

* * * * *

Up yonder on the giddy height of the Sonnen-platte where once "the wild Highland maid looked dreaming down," where later on she let herself into the depths of the gloomy abyss to rescue the be-loved one, a simple cross stands out against the blue sky. It was erected there by the village com-munity in memory of Wallburga the Vulture-maiden and Joseph the Bear-hunter—the benefactors of the whole neighbourhood.

Wally and Joseph died early, but their name lives and will be praised so long and so far as the Ache flows. The traveller who passes through the gorge late in the evening when the bell rings for vespers and the silver crescent of the moon stands above the mountains, may see an aged couple kneeling up yonder. They are Afra and Benedict Klotz, who often come down from Rofen to pray by this cross. Wally herself it was who brought their hearts together, and to-day on the brink of the grave they still bless her memory.

Below in the gorge, white, misty forms hover around the traveller and remind him of the "phantom maidens." Down from the cross there is wafted to him a lament as it were out of long-for-gotten heroic legends, a lament that the mighty as well as the feeble must fade and pass away. Still this one thought may comfort him — the heroic may die, but it cannot perish from off the earth. Under the splendid coat of mail of the Nibelungen hero, beneath the coarse peasant frocks of a Vulture-maiden and a Bear-hunter—still we meet with it again and again.

THE END.

PRINTING OFFICE OF THE PUBLISHER.

June 1889.

TAUCHNITZ EDITION.

Each volume 1 Mark 60 Pf. or 2 Francs.

This Collection of British Authors, Tauchnitz Edition, will contain the new works of the most admired English and American Writers, immediately on their appearance, with copyright for continental circulation.

Contents:

Latest Volumes:

On Circumstantial Evidence. By *Fl. Marryat*, 2 vols.
Neighbours on the Green. By Mrs. *Oliphant*, 1 vol.
Guilderoy. By *Ouida*, 2 vols.
Greifenstein. By *F. Marion Crawford*, 2 vols.
Uncle Piper of Piper's Hill. By *Tasma*, 2 vols.
A Village Tragedy. By *Margaret L. Woods*, 1 vol.
John Ward, Preacher. By *Margaret Deland*, 1 vol.
Cressy. By *Bret Harte*, 1 vol.
Under-Currents. By the Author of "Molly Bawn," 2 v.
The Outcasts, 1 vol.

Collection of British Authors.

Rev. W. Adams: Sacred Allegories 1 v.

Miss Aguilar: Home Influence 2 v. The Mother's Recompense 2 v.

Hamilton Aïdé: Rita 1 v. Carr of Carrlyon 2 v. The Marstons 2 v. In that State of Life 1 v. Morals and Mysteries 1 v. Penruddocke 2 v. "A nine Days' Wonder" 1 v. Poet and Peer 2 v. Introduced to Society 1 v.

W. Harrison Ainsworth: Windsor Castle 1 v. Saint James's 1 v. Jack Sheppard (w. portrait) 1 v. The Lancashire Witches 2 v. The Star-Chamber 2 v. The Flitch of Bacon 1 v. The Spendthrift 1 v. Mervyn Clitheroe 2 v. Ovingdean Grange 1 v. The Constable of the Tower 1 v. The Lord Mayor of London 2 v. Cardinal Pole 2 v. John Law 2 v. The Spanish Match 2 v. The Constable de Bourbon 2 v. Old Court 2 v. Myddleton Pomfret 2 v. The South-Sea Bubble 2 v. Hilary St. Ives 2 v. Talbot Harland 1 v. Tower Hill 1 v. Boscobel 2 v. The Good Old Times 2 v. Merry England 2 v. The Goldsmith's Wife 2 v. Preston Fight 2 v. Chetwynd Calverley 2 v. The Leaguer of Lathom 2 v. The Fall of Somerset 2 v. Beatrice Tyldesley 2 v. Beau Nash 2 v. Stanley Brereton 2 v.

L. M. Alcott: Little Women 2 v. Little Men 1 v. An Old-Fashioned Girl 1 v. Jo's Boys 1 v.

Mrs. Alexander: A Second Life 3 v. By Woman's Wit 1 v. Mona's Choice 2 v. A Life Interest 2 v.

Alice, Grand Duchess of Hesse (with Portrait) 2 v.

"All for Greed," Author of— All for Greed 1 v. Love the Avenger 2 v.

Thos. B. Aldrich: Marjorie Daw, etc. 1 v. Stillwater Tragedy 1 v.

L. Alldridge: By Love and Law 2 v. The World she Awoke in 2 v.

F. Anstey: The Giant's Robe 2 v. A Fallen Idol 1 v.

Matthew Arnold: Essays in Criticism 2 v.

Miss Austen: Sense and Sensibility 1 v. Mansfield Park 1 v. Pride and Prejudice 1 v. Northanger Abbey, and Persuasion 1 v. Emma 1 v.

Lady Barker: Station Life in New Zealand 1 v. Station Amusements in New Zealand 1 v. A Year's Housekeeping in South Africa 1 v. Letters to Guy & A Distant Shore—Rodrigues 1 v.

Miss Bayle's Romance 2 v.

Rev. R. H. Baynes: Lyra Anglicana, Hymns & Sacred Songs 1 v.

Lord Beaconsfield: *vide* Disraeli.

Averil Beaumont: Thornicroft's Model 2 v.

Currer Bell (Charlotte Brontë): Jane Eyre 2 v. Shirley 2 v. Villette 2 v. The Professor 1 v.

Ellis & Acton Bell: Wuthering Heights, and Agnes Grey 2 v.

Frank Lee Benedict: St. Simon's Niece 2 v.

W. Besant: The Revolt of Man 1 v. Dorothy Forster 2 v. Children of Gibeon 2 v. The World went very well then 2 v. Katharine Regina 1 v. Herr Paulus 2 v. The Inner House 1 v.

W. Besant and James Rice: The Golden Butterfly 2 v. Ready-Money Mortiboy 2 v.

W. Black: A Daughter of Heth 2 v. In Silk Attire 2 v. The strange Adventures of a Phaeton 2 v. A Princess of Thule 2 v. Kilmeny 1 v. The Maid of Killeena 1 v. Three Feathers 2 v. Lady Silverdale's Sweetheart 1 v. Madcap Violet 2 v. Green Pastures and Piccadilly 2 v. Macleod of Dare 2 v. White Wings 2 v. Sunrise 2 v. The Beautiful Wretch 1 v. Mr. Pisistratus Brown 1 v. Shandon Bells (w. portrait) 2 v. Judith Shakespeare 2 v. The Wise Women of Inverness 1 v. White Heather 2 v. Sabina Zembra 2 v. The Strange Adventures of a House-Boat 2 v. In Far Lochaber 2 v.

R. D. Blackmore: Alice Lorraine 2 v. Mary Anerley 3 v. Christowell 2 v. Tommy Upmore 2 v.

"Blackwood," Tales from— 1 v. *Second Series* 1 v.

Isa Blagden: The Woman I loved, and the Woman who loved me; A Tuscan Wedding 1 v.

Lady Blessington: Meredith

The price of each volume is 1 *Mark* 60 *Pfennig.*

1 v. Strathern 2 v. Memoirs of a Femme de Chambre 1 v. Marmaduke Herbert 2 v. Country Quarters (w. portrait) 2 v.

Rolf Bolderwood: Robbery under Arms 2 v.

Baroness Bloomfield: Reminiscences of Court & Diplomatic Life (w. Port. of Her Majesty the Queen) 2 v.

Miss Braddon: Lady Audley's Secret 2 v. Aurora Floyd 2 v. Eleanor's Victory 2 v. John Marchmont's Legacy 2 v. Henry Dunbar 2 v. The Doctor's Wife 2 v. Only a Clod 2 v. Sir Jasper's Tenant 2 v. The Lady's Mile 2 v. Rupert Godwin 2 v. Dead-Sea Fruit 2 v. Run to Earth 2 v. Fenton's Quest 2 v. The Lovels of Arden 2 v. Strangers and Pilgrims 2 v. Lucius Davoren 3 v. Taken at the Flood 3 v. Lost for Love 2 v. A Strange World 2 v. Hostages to Fortune 2 v. Dead Men's Shoes 2 v. Joshua Haggard's Daughter 2 v. Weavers and Weft 1 v. In Great Waters 1 v. An Open Verdict 3 v. Vixen 3 v. The Cloven Foot 3 v. The Story of Barbara 2 v. Just as I am 2 v. Asphodel 3 v. Mount Royal 2 v. The Golden Calf 2 v. Flower and Weed 1 v. Phantom Fortune 3 v. Under the Red Flag 1 v. Ishmael 3 v. Wyllard's Weird 3 v. One Thing Needful 2 v. Cut by the County 1 v. Like and Unlike 2 v. The Fatal Three 2 v.

Lady Brassey: A Voyage in the "Sunbeam" 2 v. Sunshine and Storm in the East 2 v. In the Trades, the Tropics, and the Roaring Forties 2 v.

The Bread-Winners 1 v.

Rev. W. Brock: A Biographical Sketch of Sir H. Havelock K.C.B. 1 v.

Shirley Brooks: The Silver Cord 3 v. Sooner or Later 3 v.

Miss Rhoda Broughton: Cometh up as a Flower 1 v. Not wisely, but too well 2 v. Red as a Rose is She 2 v. Tales for Christmas Eve 1 v. Nancy 2 v. Joan 2 v. Second Thoughts 2 v. Belinda 2 v. Doctor Cupid 2 v.

John Brown: Rab and his Friends, and other Tales 1 v.

Eliz. Barrett Browning: A Selection from her Poetry (w. portrait) 1 v. Aurora Leigh 1 v.

Robert Browning: Poetical Works (with portrait) 4 v.

Bulwer (Lord Lytton): Pelham (with portrait) 1 v. Eugene Aram 1 v. Paul Clifford 1 v. Zanoni 1 v. The Last Days of Pompeii 1 v. The Disowned 1 v. Ernest Maltravers 1 v. Alice 1 v. Eva, and the Pilgrims of the Rhine 1 v. Devereux 1 v. Godolphin, and Falkland 1 v. Rienzi 1 v. Night and Morning 1 v. The Last of the Barons 2 v. Athens 2 v. The Poems and Ballads of Schiller 1 v. Lucretia 2 v. Harold 2 v. King Arthur 2 v. The new Timon; St Stephen's 1 v. The Caxtons 2 v. My Novel 4 v. What will he do with it? 4 v. The Dramatic Works 2 v. A Strange Story 2 v. Caxtoniana 2 v. The Lost Tales of Miletus 1 v. Miscellaneous Prose Works 4 v. The Odes and Epodes of Horace 2 v. Kenelm Chillingly 4 v. The Coming Race 1 v. The Parisians 4 v. Pausanias 1 v.

Henry Lytton Bulwer (Lord Dalling): Historical Characters 2 v. The Life of Henry John Temple, Viscount Palmerston 3 v.

J. Bunyan: Pilgrim's Progress 1 v.

Buried Alone 1 v.

F. H. Burnett: Through one Administration 2 v. Little Lord Fauntleroy 1 v. Sara Crewe, etc. 1 v.

Miss Burney: Evelina 1 v.

Burns: Poet. Works (w. port.) 1 v.

Richard F. Burton: Mecca and Medina 3 v.

Mrs. B. H. Buxton: "Jennie of 'the Prince's'" 2 v. Won! 2 v. Great Grenfell Gardens 2 v. Nell—on and off the Stage 2 v. From the Wings 2 v.

Lord Byron: Poetical Works (w. portrait) 5 v.

Cameron: Across Africa 2 v.

Mrs. Campbell-Praed: Zéro 1 v. Affinities 1 v. The Head Station 2 v.

Thomas Carlyle: The French Revolution 3 v. Frederick the Great 13 v. Oliver Cromwell's Letters and Speeches 4 v. The Life of Schiller 1 v.

Alaric Carr: Treherne's Temptation 2 v.

Maria Louisa Charlesworth: Oliver of the Mill 1 v.

"Chronicles of the Schönberg-Cotta Family," Author of— Chronicles of the Schönberg-Cotta Family 2 v. The Draytons and the Davenants 2 v. On Both Sides of the Sea 2 v. Winifred Bertram 1 v. Diary of Mrs. Kitty Trevylyan 1 v. The Victory of the Vanquished 1 v. The Cottage by the Cathedral 1 v. Against the Stream 2 v. The Bertram Family 2 v. Conquering and to Conquer 1 v. Lapsed, but not Lost 1 v.

F. Power Cobbe: Re-Echoes 1 v.

Coleridge: The Poems 1 v.

C. R. Coleridge: An English Squire 2 v.

Chas. A. Collins: A Cruise upon Wheels 2 v.

Mortimer Collins: Sweet and Twenty 2 v. A Fight with Fortune 2 v.

Wilkie Collins: After Dark 1 v. Hide and Seek 2 v. A Plot in Private Life 1 v. The Woman in White 2 v. Basil 1 v. No Name 3 v. The Dead Secret 2 v. Antonina 2 v. Armadale 3 v. The Moonstone 2 v. Man and Wife 3 v. Poor Miss Finch 2 v. Miss or Mrs.? 1 v. The New Magdalen 2 v. The Frozen Deep 1 v. The Law and the Lady 2 v. The Two Destinies 1 v. My Lady's Money, etc. 1 v. The Haunted Hotel 1 v. Fallen Leaves 2 v. Jezebel's Daughter 2 v. The Black Robe 2 v. Heart and Science 2 v. "I say no" 2 v. The Evil Genius 2 v. The Guilty River, etc. 1 v. The Legacy of Cain 2 v.

"Cometh up as a Flower," Author of— *vide* Broughton.

Hugh Conway: Called Back 1 v. Bound Together 2 v. Dark Days 1 v. A Family Affair 2 v. Living or Dead 2 v.

Fenimore Cooper: The Spy (w. portrait) 1 v. The two Admirals 1 v. The Jack O'Lantern 1 v.

M. Corelli: Vendetta! 2 v. Thelma 2 v. A Romance of Two Worlds 2 v.

George L. Craik: Manual of English Literature & Language 2 v.

Mrs. Craik (Miss Mulock): John Halifax, Gentleman 2 v. The Head of the Family 2 v. A Life for a Life 2 v. A Woman's Thoughts about Women 1 v. Agatha's Husband 1 v. Romantic Tales 1 v. Domestic Stories 1 v. Mistress and Maid 1 v. The Ogilvies 1 v. Lord Erlistoun 1 v. Christian's Mistake 1 v. Bread upon the Waters 1 v. A Noble Life 1 v. Olive 2 v. Two Marriages 1 v. Studies from Life 1 v. Poems 1 v. The Woman's Kingdom 2 v. The Unkind Word 2 v. A Brave Lady 2 v. Hannah 2 v. Fair France 1 v. My Mother and I 1 v. The Little Lame Prince 1 v. Sermons out of Church 1 v. The Laurel Bush 1 v. A Legacy 2 v. Young Mrs. Jardine 2 v. His Little Mother 1 v. Plain Speaking 1 v. Miss Tommy 1 v. King Arthur: not a Love Story 1 v.

Miss G. Craik: Lost and Won 1 v. Faith Unwin's Ordeal 1 v. Leslie Tyrrell 1 v. Winifred's Wooing, etc. 1 v. Mildred 1 v. Esther Hill's Secret 2 v. Hero Trevelyan 1 v. Without Kith or Kin 2 v. Only a Butterfly 1 v. Sylvia's Choice; Theresa 2 v. Anne Warwick 1 v. Two Tales of Married Life 2 v. (Vol. I. Hard to Bear, Vol. II. *vide* M. C. Stirling.) Dorcas 2 v. Two Women 2 v.

Mrs. A. Craven: Eliane. Translated by Lady Fullerton 2 v.

F. M. Crawford: Mr. Isaacs 1 v. Doctor Claudius 1 v. To Leeward 1 v. A Roman Singer 1 v. An American Politician 1 v. Zoroaster 1 v. A Tale of a Lonely Parish 2 v. Saracinesca 2 v. Marzio's Crucifix 1 v. Paul Patoff 2 v. With the Immortals 1 v. Greifenstein 2 v.

J. W. Cross: *v.* G. Eliot's Life.

Miss Cummins: The Lamplighter 1 v. Mabel Vaughan 1 v. El Fureidîs 1 v. Haunted Hearts 1 v.

"Daily News," War Correspondence 1877 by A. Forbes, etc. 3 v.

De-Foe: Robinson Crusoe 1 v.

Margaret Deland: John Ward, Preacher 1 v.

Democracy 1 v.

Demos. A Story of English Socialism 2 v.

Charles Dickens: The Posthumous Papers of the Pickwick Club

(w. portrait) 2 v. American Notes 1 v. Oliver Twist 1 v. The Life and Adventures of Nicholas Nickleby 2 v. Sketches 1 v. The Life and Adventures of Martin Chuzzlewit 2 v. A Christmas Carol; the Chimes; the Cricket on the Hearth 1 v. Master Humphrey's Clock (Old Curiosity Shop, Barnaby Rudge, and other Tales) 3 v. Pictures from Italy 1 v. The Battle of Life; the Haunted Man 1 v. Dombey and Son 3 v. David Copperfield 3 v. Bleak House 4 v. A Child's History of England (2 v. 8° M. 2,70.) Hard Times 1 v. Little Dorrit 4 v. A Tale of two Cities 2 v. Hunted Down; The Uncommercial Traveller 1 v. Great Expectations 2 v. Christmas Stories 1 v. Our Mutual Friend 4 v. Somebody's Luggage; Mrs. Lirriper's Lodgings; Mrs. Lirriper's Legacy 1 v. Doctor Marigold's Prescriptions; Mugby Junction 1 v. No Thoroughfare 1 v. The Mystery of Edwin Drood 2 v. The Mudfog Papers 1 v. *Vide* Household Words, Novels and Tales, and John Forster.

Charles Dickens: The Letters of Charles Dickens edited by his Sister-in-law and his eldest Daughter 4 v.

B. Disraeli (Lord Beaconsfield): Coningsby 1 v. Sybil 1 v. Contarini Fleming (w. portrait) 1 v. Alroy 1 v. Tancred 2 v. Venetia 2 v. Vivian Grey 2 v. Henrietta Temple 1 v. Lothair 2 v. Endymion 2 v.

W. Hepworth Dixon: Personal History of Lord Bacon 1 v. The Holy Land, 2 v. New America 2 v. Spiritual Wives 2 v. Her Majesty's Tower 4 v. Free Russia 2 v. History of two Queens 6 v. White Conquest 2 v. Diana, Lady Lyle 2 v.

The Earl and the Doctor: South Sea Bubbles 1 v.

Mrs. Edwardes: Archie Lovell 2 v. Steven Lawrence, Yeoman 2 v. Ought we to Visit her? 2 v. A Vagabond Heroine 1 v. Leah: A Woman of Fashion 2 v. A Blue-Stocking 1 v. Jet: Her Face or Her Fortune? 1 v. Vivian the Beauty 1 v. A Ballroom Repentance 2 v. A Girton Girl 2 v. A Playwright's Daughter & Bertie Griffiths 1 v.

Miss Amelia B. Edwards:

Barbara's History 2 v. Miss Carew 2 v. Hand and Glove 1 v. Half a Million of Money 2 v. Debenham's Vow 2 v. In the Days of my Youth 2 v. Untrodden Peaks and unfrequented Valleys 1 v. Monsieur Maurice 1 v. Black Forest 1 v. A Poetry-Book of Elder Poets 1 v. A Thousand Miles up the Nile 2 v. A Poetry-Book of Modern Poets 1 v. Lord Brackenbury 2 v.

Miss M. Betham-Edwards: The Sylvestres 1 v. Felicia 2 v. Brother Gabriel 2 v. Forestalled 1 v. Exchange no Robbery 1 v. Disarmed 1 v. Doctor Jacob 1 v. Pearla 1 v. Next of Kin Wanted 1 v. The Parting of the Ways 1 v.

Barbara Elbon: Bethesda 2 v.

George Eliot: Scenes of Clerical Life 2 v. Adam Bede 2 v. The Mill on the Floss 2 v. Silas Marner 1 v. Romola 2 v. Felix Holt 2 v. Daniel Deronda 4 v. The Lifted Veil and Brother Jacob 1 v. Impressions of Theophrastus Such 1 v. Essays 1 v.

George Eliot's Life as related in her Letters and Journals. Arranged and ed. by her Husband J. W. Cross 4 v.

Mrs. Elliot: Diary of an Idle Woman in Italy 2 v. Old Court Life in France 2 v. The Italians 2 v. The Diary of an Idle Woman in Sicily 1 v. Pictures of Old Rome 1 v. Diary of an Idle Woman in Spain 2 v. The Red Cardinal 1 v.

H. Erroll: An Ugly Duckling 1 v.

Essays and Reviews 1 v.

Estelle Russell 2 v.

J. H. Ewing: Jackanapes, etc. 1 v.

Expiated 2 v.

G. M. Fenn: The Parson o' Dumford 2 v. The Clerk of Portwick 2 v.

Fielding: Tom Jones 2 v.

Five Centuries of the English Language and Literature 1 v.

George Fleming: Kismet 1 v. Andromeda 2 v.

A. Forbes: My Experiences of the War between France and Germany 2 v. Soldiering and Scribbling 1 v. See also "Daily News," War Correspondence.

Mrs. Forrester: Viva 2 v.

Rhona 2 v. Roy and Viola 2 v. My Lord and My Lady 2 v. I have Lived and Loved 2 v. June 2 v. Omnia Vanitas 1 v. Although he was a Lord, etc. 1 v. Corisande, etc. 1 v. Once Again 2 v.

John Forster: Life of Charles Dickens 6 v. Life and Times of Oliver Goldsmith 2 v.

Jessie Fothergill: The First Violin 2 v. Probation 2 v. Made or Marred and "One of Three" 1 v. Kith and Kin 2 v. Peril 2 v. Borderland 2 v.

"Found Dead," Author of— *vide* James Payn.

Caroline Fox: Memories of Old Friends from her Journals, edited by Horace N. Pym 2 v.

Frank Fairlegh 2 v.

E. A. Freeman: The Growth of the English Constitution 1 v. Select Historical Essays 1 v.

J. A. Froude: Oceana 1 v.

Lady G. Fullerton: Ellen Middleton 1 v. Grantley Manor 2 v. Lady-Bird 2 v. Too Strange not to be True 2 v. Constance Sherwood 2 v. A stormy Life 2 v. Mrs. Gerald's Niece 2 v. The Notary's Daughter 1 v. The Lilies of the Valley 1 v. The Countess de Bonneval 1 v. Rose Leblanc 1 v. Seven Stories 1 v. The Life of Luisa de Carvajal 1 v. A Will and a Way 2 v. Eliane 2 v. (*vide* Craven). Laurentia 1 v.

Mrs. Gaskell: Mary Barton 1 v. Ruth 2 v. North and South 1 v. Lizzie Leigh 1 v. The Life of Charlotte Brontë 2 v. Lois the Witch 1 v. Sylvia's Lovers 2 v. A Dark Night's Work 1 v. Wives and Daughters 3 v. Cranford 1 v. Cousin Phillis, and other Tales 1 v.

G. Hawthorne *v.* "Miss Molly."

Agnes Giberne: The Curate's Home 1 v.

Right Hon. W. E. Gladstone: Rome and the newest Fashions in Religion 1 v. Bulgarian Horrors: Russia in Turkistan 1 v. The Hellenic Factor in the Eastern Problem 1 v.

Goldsmith: Select Works: The Vicar of Wakefield; Poems; Dramas (w. portrait) 1 v.

E. J. Goodman: Too Curious 1 v.

Major-Gen. C. G. Gordon's Journals, at Kartoum. Introduction and Notes by A. E. Hake (with eighteen Illustrations) 2 v.

Mrs. Gore: Castles in the Air 1 v. The Dean's Daughter 2 v. Progress and Prejudice 2 v. Mammon 2 v. A Life's Lessons 2 v. The two Aristocracies 2 v. Heckington 2 v.

Miss Grant: Victor Lescar 2 v. The Sun-Maid 2 v. My Heart's in the Highlands 2 v. Artiste 2 v. Prince Hugo 2 v. Cara Roma 2 v.

Maxwell Gray: The Silence of Dean Maitland 2 v.

W. A. Baillie Grohman: Tyrol and the Tyrolese 1 v.

A. Clavering Gunter: Mr. Barnes of New York 1 v.

"Guy Livingstone," Author of—Guy Livingstone 1 v. Sword and Gown 1 v. Barren Honour 1 v. Border and Bastille 1 v. Maurice Dering 1 v. Sans Merci 2 v. Breaking a Butterfly 2 v. Anteros 2 v. Hagarene 2 v.

J. Habberton: Helen's Babies & Other People's Children 1 v. The Bowsham Puzzle 1 v. One Tramp; Mrs. Mayburn's Twins 1 v.

H. Rider Haggard: King Solomon's Mines 1 v. She 2 v. Jess 2 v. Allan Quatermain 2 v. The Witch's Head 2 v. Maiwa's Revenge 1 v. Mr. Meeson's Will 1 v. Colonel Quaritch, V.C. 2 v.

Hake: *v.* Gordon's Journals.

Mrs. S. C. Hall: Can Wrong be Right? 1 v. Marian 2 v.

Thomas Hardy: The Hand of Ethelberta 2 v. Far from the Madding Crowd 2 v. The Return of the Native 2 v. The Trumpet-Major 2 v. A Laodicean 2 v. Two on a Tower 2 v. A Pair of Blue Eyes 2 v.

Agnes Harrison: Martin's Vineyard 1 v.

Bret Harte: Prose and Poetry (Tales of the Argonauts; Spanish and American Legends: Condensed Novels; Civic and Character Sketches; Poems) 2 v. Idyls of the Foothills 1 v. Gabriel

Conroy 2 v. Two Men of Sandy Bar 1 v. Thankful Blossom 1 v. The Story of a Mine 1 v. Drift from Two Shores 1 v. An Heiress of Red Dog 1 v. The Twins of Table Mountain, etc. 1 v. Jeff Briggs's Love Story, etc. 1 v. Flip, etc. 1 v. On the Frontier 1 v. By Shore and Sedge 1 v. Maruja 1 v. Snow-bound at Eagle's 1 v. The Crusade of the "Excelsior" 1 v. A Millionaire of Rough-and-Ready, etc. 1 v. Captain Jim's Friend, etc. 1 v. Cressy 1 v.

Sir H. Havelock: *vide* Rev. W. Brock.

N. Hawthorne: The Scarlet Letter 1 v. Transformation 2 v. Passages from the English Note-Books 2 v.

"Heir of Redclyffe," Author of— *vide* Yonge.

Sir Arthur Helps: Friends in Council 2 v. Ivan de Biron 2 v.

Mrs. Hemans: The Select Poetical Works 1 v.

Admiral Hobart Pasha: Sketches from my Life 1 v.

Mrs. Cashel Hoey: A Golden Sorrow 2 v. Out of Court 2 v.

Oliver Wendell Holmes: The Autocrat of the Breakfast-Table 1 v. The Professor at the Breakfast-Table 1 v. The Poet at the Breakfast-Table 1 v.

Household Words conducted by Ch. Dickens. 1851-56. 36 v. NOVELS and TALES reprinted from Household Words by Ch. Dickens. 1856-59. 11 v.

How to be Happy though Married 1 v.

Miss Howard: One Summer 1 v. Aunt Serena 1 v. Guenn 2 v. Tony, the Maid, etc. 1 v.

W. D. Howells: A Foregone Conclusion 1 v. The Lady of the Aroostook 1 v. A Modern Instance 2 v. The Undiscovered Country 1 v. Venetian Life (w. portr.) 1 v. Italian Journeys 1 v. A Chance Acquaintance 1 v. Their Wedding Journey 1 v. A Fearful Responsibility, etc. 1 v. A Woman's Reason 2 v. Dr. Breen's Practice 1 v. The Rise of Silas Lapham 2 v.

Thos. Hughes: Tom Brown's School Days 1 v.

Jean Ingelow: Off the Skelligs 3 v. Poems 2 v. Fated to be Free 2 v. Sarah de Berenger 2 v. Don John 2 v.

J. H. Ingram: *vide* E. A. Poe.

Washington Irving: Sketch Book (w. portrait) 1 v. Life of Mahomet 1 v. Successors of Mahomet 1 v. Oliver Goldsmith 1 v. Chronicles of Wolfert's Roost 1 v. Life of George Washington 5 v.

Helen Jackson: Ramona 2 v.

G. P. R. James: Morley Ernstein (w. portrait) 1 v. Forest Days 1 v. The False Heir 1 v. Arabella Stuart 1 v. Rose d'Albret 1 v. Arrah Neil 1 v. Agincourt 1 v. The Smuggler 1 v. The Step-Mother 2 v. Beauchamp 1 v. Heidelberg 1 v. The Gipsy 1 v. The Castle of Ehrenstein 1 v. Darnley 1 v. Russell 2 v. The Convict 2 v. Sir Theodore Broughton 2 v.

Henry James: The American 2 v. The Europeans 1 v. Daisy Miller 1 v. Roderick Hudson 2 v. The Madonna of the Future, etc. 1 v. Eugene Pickering, etc. 1 v. Confidence 1 v. Washington Square 2 v. The Portrait of a Lady 3 v. Foreign Parts 1 v. French Poets and Novelists 1 v. The Siege of London, etc. 1 v. Portraits of Places 1 v. A Little Tour in France 1 v.

J. Cordy Jeaffreson: A Book about Doctors 2 v. A Woman in Spite of herself 2 v. The Real Lord Byron 3 v.

Mrs. Jenkin: "Who Breaks— Pays" 1 v. Skirmishing 1 v. Once and Again 2 v. Two French Marriages 2 v. Within an Ace 1 v. Jupiter's Daughters 1 v.

Edward Jenkins: Ginx's Baby: Lord Bantam 2 v.

"Jennie of 'the Prince's,'" Author of— *vide* Mrs. Buxton.

Douglas Jerrold: The History of St. Giles and St. James 2 v. Men of Character 2 v.

"John Halifax," Author of— *vide* Mrs. Craik.

"Johnny Ludlow," Author of— *vide* Mrs. Wood.

Johnson: The Lives of the English Poets 2 v.

Emily Jolly: Colonel Dacre 2 v.

"Joshua Davidson," Author of— *vide* E. Lynn Linton.

Miss Kavanagh: Nathalie 2 v. Daisy Burns 2 v. Grace Lee 2 v. Rachel Gray 1 v. Adèle 3 v. A Summer and Winter in the Two Sicilies 2 v. Seven Years 2 v. French Women of Letters 1 v. English Women of Letters 1 v. Queen Mab 2 v. Beatrice 2 v. Sybil's Second Love 2 v. Dora 2 v. Silvia 2 v. Bessie 2 v. John Dorrien 3 v. Two Lilies 2 v. Forget-me-nots 2 v.

Annie Keary: Oldbury 2 v. Castle Daly 2 v.

Elsa D'Esterre - Keeling: Three Sisters 1 v. A Laughing Philosopher 1 v. The Professor's Wooing 1 v.

Kempis: *v.* Thomas a Kempis.

R. B. Kimball: Saint Leger 1 v. Romance of Student Life abroad 1 v. Undercurrents 1 v. Was he Successful? 1 v. To-Day in New-York 1 v.

A. W. Kinglake: Eothen 1 v. Invasion of the Crimea 14 v.

Charles Kingsley: Yeast 1 v. Westward ho! 2 v. Two Years ago 2 v. Hypatia 2 v. Alton Locke 1 v. Hereward the Wake 2 v. At Last 2 v.

Charles Kingsley: His Letters and Memories of his Life edited by his Wife 2 v.

Henry Kingsley: Ravenshoe 2 v. Austin Elliot 1 v. The Recollections of Geoffry Hamlyn 2 v. The Hillyars and the Burtons 2 v. Leighton Court 1 v. Valentin 1 v. Oakshott Castle 1 v. Reginald Hetherege 2 v. The Grange Garden 2 v.

May Laffan: Flitters, Tatters, and the Counsellor, etc. 1 v.

Charles Lamb: The Essays of Elia and Eliana 1 v.

Mary Langdon: Ida May 1 v.

"Last of the Cavaliers," Author of—Last of the Cavaliers 2 v. The Gain of a Loss 2 v.

Hon. E. Lawless: Hurrish 1 v.

Leaves from the Journal of our Life in the Highlands from 1848 to 1861, 1 v. More Leaves from the Journal of a Life in the Highlands from 1862 to 1882, 1 v.

Holme Lee: *vide* Miss Parr.

S. Le Fanu: Uncle Silas 2 v. Guy Deverell 2 v.

Mark Lemon: Wait for the End 2 v. Loved at Last 2 v. Falkner Lyle 2 v. Leyton Hall 2 v. Golden Fetters 2 v.

Charles Lever: The O'Donoghue 1 v. The Knight of Gwynne 3 v. Arthur O'Leary 2 v. The Confessions of Harry Lorrequer 2 v. Charles O'Malley 3 v. Tom Burke of "Ours" 3 v. Jack Hinton 2 v. The Daltons 4 v. The Dodd Family abroad 3 v. The Martins of Cro' Martin 3 v. The Fortunes of Glencore 2 v. Roland Cashel 3 v. Davenport Dunn 3 v. Con Cregan 2 v. One of Them 2 v. Maurice Tiernay 2 v. Sir Jasper Carew 2 v. Barrington 2 v. A Day's Ride: a Life's Romance 2 v. Luttrell of Arran 2 v. Tony Butler 2 v. Sir Brook Fossbrooke 2 v. The Bramleighs of Bishop's Folly 2 v. A Rent in a Cloud 1 v. That Boy of Norcott's 1 v. St. Patrick's Eve; Paul Gosslett's Confessions 1 v. Lord Kilgobbin 2 v.

G. H. Lewes: Ranthorpe 1 v. Physiology of Common Life 2 v. On Actors and the Art of Acting 1 v.

E. Lynn Linton: Joshua Davidson 1 v. Patricia Kemball 2 v. The Atonement of Leam Dundas 2 v. The World well Lost 2 v. Under which Lord? 2 v. With a Silken Thread etc. 1 v. Todhunters' at Loanin' Head etc. 1 v. "My Love!" 2 v. The Girl of the Period, etc. 1 v. Ione 2 v.

Laurence W. M. Lockhart: Mine is Thine 2 v.

Longfellow: Poetical Works (w. portrait) 3 v. The Divine Comedy of Dante Alighieri 3 v. The New-England Tragedies 1 v. The Divine Tragedy 1 v. Three Books of Song 1 v. The Masque of Pandora 1 v.

M. Lonsdale: Sister Dora 1 v.

A Lost Battle 2 v.

Lutfullah: Autobiography of Lutfullah, by Eastwick 1 v.

Lord Lytton: *vide* Bulwer.

R. Lord Lytton (Owen Meredith): Poems 2 v. Fables in Song 2 v.

Lord Macaulay: History of England) w. portrait) 10 v. Critical and Historical Essays 5 v. Lays of Ancient Rome 1 v. Speeches 2 v. Biographical Essays 1 v. William Pitt, Atterbury 1 v. (See also Trevelyan).

Justin McCarthy: Waterdale Neighbours 2 v. Lady Disdain 2 v. Miss Misanthrope 2 v. A History of our own Times 5 v. Donna Quixote 2 v. A short History of our own Times 2 v. A History of the Four Georges vol. 1.

George MacDonald: Alec Forbes of Howglen 2 v. Annals of a Quiet Neighbourhood 2 v. David Elginbrod 2 v. The Vicar's Daughter 2 v. Malcolm 2 v. St. George and St. Michael 2 v. The Marquis of Lossie 2 v. Sir Gibbie 2 v. Mary Marston 2 v. The Gifts of the Child Christ, etc. 1 v. The Princess and Curdie 1 v.

Mrs. Mackarness: Sunbeam Stories 1 v. A Peerless Wife 2 v. A Mingled Yarn 2 v.

Charles McKnight: Old Fort Duquesne 2 v.

Norman Macleod: The old Lieutenant and his Son 1 v.

Mrs. Macquoid: Patty 2 v. Miriam's Marriage 2 v. Pictures across the Channel 2 v. Too Soon 1 v. My Story 2 v. Diane 2 v. Beside the River 2 v. A Faithful Lover 2 v.

"Mademoiselle Mori," Author of— Mademoiselle Mori 2 v. Denise 1 v. Madame Fontenoy 1 v. On the Edge of the Storm 1 v. The Atelier du Lys 2 v. In the Olden Time 2 v.

Lord Mahon: *vide* Stanhope.

E. S. Maine: Scarscliff Rocks 2 v.

Lucas Malet: Colonel Enderby's Wife 2 v.

Lord Malmesbury: Memoirs of an Ex-Minister 3 v.

R. Blachford Mansfield: The Log of the Water Lily 1 v.

Mark Twain: *vide* Twain.

Marmorne 1 v.

Capt. Marryat: Jacob Faithful (w. portrait) 1 v. Percival Keene 1 v. Peter Simple 1 v. Japhet 1 v. Monsieur Violet 1 v. The Settlers 1 v. The Mission 1 v. The Privateer's-Man 1 v. The Children of the New-Forest 1 v. Valerie 1 v. Mr. Midshipman Easy 1 v. The King's Own 1 v.

Florence Marryat: Love's Conflict 2 v. For Ever and Ever 2 v. The Confessions of Gerald Estcourt 2 v. Nelly Brooke 2 v. Véronique 2 v. Petronel 2 v. Her Lord and Master 2 v. The Prey of the Gods 1 v. Life of Capt. Marryat 1 v. Mad Dumaresq 2 v. No Intentions 2 v. Fighting the Air 2 v. A Star and a Heart 1 v. The Poison of Asps 1 v. A Lucky Disappointment 1 v. My own Child 2 v. Her Father's Name 2 v. A Harvest of Wild Oats 2 v. A Little Stepson 1 v. Written in Fire 2 v. Her World against a Lie 2 v. A Broken Blossom 2 v. The Root of all Evil 2 v. The Fair-haired Alda 2 v. With Cupid's Eyes 2 v. My Sister the Actress 2 v. Phyllida 2 v. How They Loved Him 2 v. Facing the Footlights (w. portrait) 2 v. A Moment of Madness 1 v. The Ghost of Charlotte Cray, etc. 1 v. Peeress and Player 2 v. Under the Lilies and Roses 2 v. The Heart of Jane Warner 2 v. The Heir Presumptive 2 v. The Master Passion 2 v. Spiders of Society 2 v. Driven to Bay 2 v. A Daughter of the Tropics 2 v. Gentleman and Courtier 2 v. On Circumstantial Evidence 2 v.

Mrs. Marsh: Ravenscliffe 2 v. Emilia Wyndham 2 v. Castle Avon 2 v. Aubrey 2 v. The Heiress of Haughton 2 v. Evelyn Marston 2 v. The Rose of Ashurst 2 v.

Emma Marshall: Mrs. Mainwaring's Journal 1 v. Benvenuta 1 v. Lady Alice 1 v. Dayspring 1 v. Life's Aftermath 1 v. In the East Country 1 v. No. XIII; or, The Story of the Lost Vestal 1 v. In Four Reigns 1 v. On the Banks of the Ouse 1 v. In the City of Flowers 1 v.

H. Mathers: "Cherry Ripe!" 2 v. "Land o' the Leal" 1 v. My Lady Green Sleeves 2 v. As he comes up the

Stair, etc. v v. Sam's Sweetheart 2 v.
Eyre's Acquittal 2 v. Found Out 1 v.
Murder or Manslaughter? 1 v. The
Fashion of this World (80 Pf.).

Colonel Maurice: The Bal-
ance of Military Power in Europe 1 v.

"Mehalah," Author of—
Mehalah 1 v. John Herring 2 v. Court
Royal 2 v.

WhyteMelville: Kate Coventry
1 v. Holmby House 2 v. Digby Grand
1 v. Good for Nothing 2 v. The Queen's
Maries 2 v. The Gladiators 2 v. The
Brookes of Bridlemere 2 v. Cerise 2 v.
The Interpreter 2 v. The White Rose 2 v.
M. or N. 1 v. Contraband; or A Losing
Hazard 1 v. Sarchedon 2 v. Uncle John
2 v. Katerfelto 1 v. Sister Louise 1 v.
Rosine 1 v. Roy's Wife 2 v. Black but
Comely 2 v. Riding Recollections 1 v.

George Meredith: The Or-
deal of Feverel 2 v. Beauchamp's
Career 2 v. The Tragic Comedians 1 v.

Owen Meredith: *vide* Robert
Lord Lytton.

Milton: Poetical Works 1 v.

"Miss Molly," Author of—
Geraldine Hawthorne 1 v.

"Molly Bawn," Author of—
Molly Bawn 2 v. Mrs. Geoffrey 2 v.
Faith and Unfaith 2 v. Portia 2 v.
Loÿs, Lord Berresford, etc. 1 v. Her
First Appearance, etc. 1 v. Phyllis 2 v.
Rossmoyne 2 v. Doris 2 v. A Maiden
all Forlorn, etc. 1 v. A Passive Crime 1 v.
Green Pleasure and Grey Grief 2 v.
A Mental Struggle 2 v. Her Week's
Amusement 1 v. Lady Branksmere 2 v.
Lady Valworth's Diamonds 1 v. A
Modern Circe 2 v. Marvel 2 v. The Hon.
Mrs. Vereker 1 v. Under-Currents 2 v.

Miss Montgomery: Misunder-
stood 1 v. Thrown Together 2 v.
Thwarted 1 v. Wild Mike 1 v. Seaforth
2 v. The Blue Veil 1 v. Transformed
1 v. The Fisherman's Daughter 1 v.

Moore: Poet. Works (w. port.) 5 v.

Lady Morgan's Memoirs 3 v.

Henry Morley: Of English
Literature in the Reign of Victoria.
With Facsimiles of the Signatures of
Authors in the Tauchnitz Ed. [v. 2000].

William Morris: Poems 1 v.

D. C. Murray: Rainbow Gold 2 v.

E. C. Grenville:Murray: The
Member for Paris 2 v. Young Brown
2 v. The Boudoir Cabal 3 v. French
Pictures in English Chalk (1st Series)
2 v. The Russians of To-day 1 v. French
Pictures in English Chalk (2nd Series)
2 v. Strange Tales 1 v. That Artful
Vicar 2 v. Six Months in the Ranks 1 v.
People I have met 1 v.

"My little Lady," Author of—
vide E. Frances Poynter.

New Testament [v. 1000].

Mrs. Newby: Common Sense 2 v.

Dr. J. H. Newman: Callista 1 v.

"Nina Balatka," Author of—
vide Anthony Trollope.

"No Church," Author of—No
Church 2 v. Owen:—a Waif 2 v.

Lady Noel: From Generation to
Generation 1 v. Hithersea Mere 2 v.

Hon. Mrs. Norton: Stuart of
Dunleath 2 v. Lost and Saved 2 v.
Old Sir Douglas 2 v.

W. E. Norris: My Friend Jim 1 v.
A Bachelor's Blunder 2 v. Major and
Minor 2 v. The Rogue 2 v.

Novels and Tales *vide* Household Words.

Not Easily Jealous 2 v.

L. Oliphant: Altiora Peto 2 v.
Masollam 2 v.

Mrs. Oliphant: Passages in the
Life of Mrs. Margaret Maitland of Sun-
nyside 1 v. The Last of the Mortimers
2 v. Agnes 2 v. Madonna Mary 2 v.
The Minister's Wife 2 v. The Rector,
and the Doctor's Family 1 v. Salem
Chapel 2 v. The Perpetual Curate 2 v.
Miss Marjoribanks 2 v. Ombra 2 v. Me-
moir of Count de Montalembert 2 v.
May 2 v. Innocent 2 v. For Love and
Life 2 v. A Rose in June 1 v. The Story
of Valentine and his Brother 2 v.
Whiteladies 2 v. The Curate in Charge
1 v. Phœbe, Junior 2 v. Mrs. Arthur 2 v.
Carità 2 v. Young Musgrave 2 v. The
Primrose Path 2 v. Within the Precincts
3 v. The greatest Heiress in England

The price of each volume is 1 *Mark* 60 *Pfennig.*

2 v. He that will not when he may 2 v. Harry Joscelyn 2 v. In Trust 2 v. It was a Lover and his Lass 3 v. The Ladies Lindores 3 v. Hester 3 v. The Wizard's Son 3 v. A Country Gentleman 2 v. Neighbours on the Green 1 v.

Ossian: Poems 1 v.

Ouida: Idalia 2 v. Tricotrin 2 v. Puck 2 v. Chandos 2 v. Strathmore 2 v. Under two Flags 2 v. Folle-Farine 2 v. A Leaf in the Storm; A Dog of Flanders, etc. 1 v. Cecil Castlemaine's Gage 1 v. Madame la Marquise 1 v. Pascarèl 2 v. Held in Bondage 2 v. Two little Wooden Shoes 1 v. Signa (w. portrait) 3 v. In a Winter City 1 v. Ariadnê 2 v. Friendship 2 v. Moths 3 v. Pipistrello 1 v. A Village Commune 2 v. In Maremma 3 v. Bimbi 1 v. Wanda 3 v. Frescoes, etc. 1 v. Princess Napraxine 3 v. A Rainy June (60 Pf.). Othmar 3 v. Don Gesualdo (60 Pf.). A House Party 1 v. Guilderoy 2 v.

The Outcasts 1 v.

Miss Parr (Holme Lee): Basil Godfrey's Caprice 2 v. For Richer, for Poorer 2 v. The Beautiful Miss Barrington 2 v. Her Title of Honour 1 v. Echoes of a Famous Year 1 v. Katherine's Trial 1 v. Bessie Fairfax 2 v. Ben Milner's Wooing 1 v. Straightforward 2 v. Mrs. Denys of Cote 2 v. A Poor Squire 1 v.

Mrs. Parr: Dorothy Fox 1 v. The Prescotts of Pamphillon 2 v. Gosau Smithy 1 v. Robin 2 v. Loyalty George 2 v.

"Paul Ferroll," Author of— Paul Ferroll 1 v. Year after Year 1 v. Why Paul Ferroll killed his Wife 1 v.

James Payn: Found Dead 1 v. Gwendoline's Harvest 1 v. Like Father, like Son 2 v. Not Wooed, but Won 2 v. Cecil's Tryst 1 v. A Woman's Vengeance 2 v. Murphy's Master 1 v. In the Heart of a Hill 1 v. At Her Mercy 2 v. The Best of Husbands 2 v. Walter's Word 2 v. Halves 2 v. Fallen Fortunes 2 v. What He cost Her 2 v. By Proxy 2 v. Less Black than we're Painted 2 v. Under one Roof 2 v. High Spirits 1 v. High Spirits (Second Series) 1 v. A Confidential Agent 2 v. From Exile 2 v. A Grape from a Thorn 2 v.

Some Private Views 1 v. For Cash Only 2 v. Kit: A Memory 2 v. The Canon's Ward 2 v. Some Literary Recollections 1 v. The Talk of the Town 1 v. The Luck of the Darrells 2 v. The Heir of the Ages 2 v. Holiday Tasks 1 v. Glow-Worm Tales (First Series) 1 v. Glow-Worm Tales (Second Series) 1 v. A Prince of the Blood 2 v. The Mystery of Mirbridge 2 v.

Miss Fr. M. Peard: One Year 2 v. The Rose-Garden 1 v. Unawares 1 v. Thorpe Regis 1 v. A Winter Story 1 v. A Madrigal 1 v. Cartouche 1 v. Mother Molly 1 v. Schloss and Town 2 v. Contradictions 2 v. Near Neighbours 1 v. Alicia Tennant 1 v. Madame's Grand-Daughter 1 v.

Bishop Percy: Reliques of Ancient English Poetry 3 v.

F. C. Philips: As in a Looking Glass 1 v. The Dean and his Daughter 1 v. The Strange Adventures of Lucy Smith 1 v. A Lucky Young Woman 1 v. Jack and Three Jills 1 v. Little Mrs. Murray 1 v.

E. A. Poe: Poems and Essays. Ed. with a new Memoir by J. H. Ingram 1 v. Tales. Ed. by J. H. Ingram 1 v.

Pope: Select Poetical Works (w. portrait) 1 v.

E. Frances Poynter: My little Lady 2 v. Ersilia 2 v. Among the Hills 1 v. Madame de Presnel 1 v.

Mrs. Praed: *vide* Campbell-Praed.

Mrs. E. Prentiss: Stepping Heavenward 1 v.

The Prince Consort's Speeches and Addresses 1 v.

Horace N. Pym: *vide* C. Fox.

W. F. Rae: Westward by Rail 1 v.

Charles Reade: "It is never too late to mend" 2 v. "Love me little love me long" 1 v. The Cloister and the Hearth 2 v. Hard Cash 3 v. Put Yourself in his Place 2 v. A Terrible Temptation 2 v. Peg Woffington 1 v. Christie Johnstone 1 v. A Simpleton 2 v. The Wandering Heir 1 v. A Woman-Hater 2 v. Readiana 1 v. Singleheart and Doubleface 1 v.

"Recommended to Mercy," Author of—Recommended to Mercy 2 v. Zoe's 'Brand' 2 v.

James Rice: *vide* W. Besant.

Alfred Bate Richards: So very Human 3 v.

Richardson: Clarissa Harlowe 4 v.

Mrs. Riddell (F. G. Trafford): George Geith of Fen Court 2 v. Maxwell Drewitt 2 v. The Race for Wealth 2 v. Far above Rubies 2 v. The Earl's Promise 2 v. Mortomley's Estate 2 v.

Rev. W. Robertson: Sermons 4 v.

Charles H. Ross: The Pretty Widow 1 v. A London Romance 2 v.

Dante Gabriel Rossetti: Poems 1 v. Ballads and Sonnets 1 v.

J. Ruffini: Lavinia 2 v. Doctor Antonio 1 v. Lorenzo Benoni 1 v. Vincenzo 2 v. A Quiet Nook 1 v. The Paragreens on a Visit to Paris 1 v. Carlino and other Stories 1 v.

W. Clark Russell: A Sailor's Sweetheart 2 v. The "Lady Maud" 2 v. A Sea Queen 2 v.

G. A. Sala: The Seven Sons of Mammon 2 v.

John Saunders: Israel Mort, Overman 2 v. The Shipowner's Daughter 2 v. A Noble Wife 2 v.

K. Saunders: Joan Merryweather, etc. 1 v. Gideon's Rock 1 v. The High Mills 2 v. Sebastian 1 v.

Sir W. Scott: Waverley (w. port.) 1 v. The Antiquary 1 v. Ivanhoe 1 v. Kenilworth 1 v. Quentin Durward 1 v. Old Mortality 1 v. Guy Mannering 1 v. Rob Roy 1 v. The Pirate 1 v. The Fortunes of Nigel 1 v. The Black Dwarf; A Legend of Montrose 1 v. The Bride of Lammermoor 1 v. The Heart of Mid-Lothian 2 v. The Monastery 1 v. The Abbot 1 v. Peveril of the Peak 2 v. The Poetical Works 2 v. Woodstock 1 v. The Fair Maid of Perth 1 v. Anne of Geierstein 1 v.

Professor Seeley: Life and Times of Stein 4 v. The Expansion of England 1 v.

Miss Sewell: Amy Herbert 2 v. Ursula 2 v. A Glimpse of the World 2 v. The Journal of a Home Life 2 v. After Life 2 v. The Experience of Life; or, Aunt Sarah 2 v.

Shakespeare: Plays and Poems (w. portr.) *(2nd Edition)* compl. 7 v. *Shakespeare's* Plays may also be had in 37 numbers, at M. 0,30. each number. Doubtful Plays 1 v.

Shelley: A Selection from his Poems 1 v.

Nathan Sheppard: Shut up in Paris *(Second Edition, enlarged)* 1 v.

Sheridan: Dramatic Works 1 v.

J. Henry Shorthouse: John Inglesant 2 v.

Smollett: The Adventures of Roderick Random 1 v. The Expedition of Humphry Clinker 1 v. The Adventures of Peregrine Pickle 2 v.

Society in London. By a Foreign Resident 1 v.

Earl Stanhope (Lord Mahon): History of England 7 v. The Reign of Queen Anne 2 v.

Sterne: The Life and Opinions of Tristram Shandy 1 v. A Sentimental Journey (w. portrait) 1 v.

Robert Louis Stevenson: Treasure Island 1 v. Dr. Jekyll and Mr. Hyde, etc. 1 v. Kidnapped 1 v. The Black Arrow 1 v.

"Still Waters," Author of— Still Waters 1 v. Dorothy 1 v. De Cressy 1 v. Uncle Ralph 1 v. Maiden Sisters 1 v. Martha Brown 1 v. Vanessa 1 v.

M. C. Stirling: Two Tales of Married Life 2 v. Vol. II, A True Man, Vol. I. *vide* G. M. Craik.

"The Story of Elizabeth," Author of— *v.* Miss Thackeray.

Mrs. H. Beecher Stowe: Uncle Tom's Cabin (w. portrait) 2 v. A Key to Uncle Tom's Cabin 2 v. Dred 2 v. The Minister's Wooing 1 v. Oldtown Folks 2 v.

"Sunbeam Stories," Author of— *vide* Mackarness.

Swift: Gulliver's Travels 1 v.

J. A. Symonds: Sketches in Italy 1 v. New Italian Sketches 1 v.

Tasma: Uncle Piper of Piper's Hill 2 v.

Baroness Tautphoeus: Cyrilla 2 v. The Initials 2 v. Quits 2 v. At Odds 2 v.

Colonel Meadows Taylor: Tara: a Mahratta Tale 3 v.

Templeton: Diary & Notes 1 v.

Lord Tennyson: Poetical Works 7 v. Queen Mary 1 v. Harold 1 v. Ballads and other Poems 1 v. Becket; The Cup; The Falcon 1 v. Locksley Hall, etc. 1 v.

W. M. Thackeray: Vanity Fair 3 v. The History of Pendennis 3 v. Miscellanies 8 v. The History of Henry Esmond 2 v. The English Humourists 1 v. The Newcomes 4 v. The Virginians 4 v. The Four Georges; Lovel the Widower 1 v. The Adventures of Philip 2 v. Denis Duval 1 v. Roundabout Papers 2 v. Catherine 1 v. The Irish Sketch Book 2 v. The Paris Sketch Book (w. portrait) 2 v.

Miss Thackeray: The Story of Elizabeth 1 v. The Village on the Cliff 1 v. Old Kensington 2 v. Bluebeard's Keys 1 v. Five Old Friends 1 v. Miss Angel 1 v. Out of the World 1 v. Fulham Lawn 1 v. From an Island 1 v. Da Capo 1 v. Madame de Sévigné 1 v. A Book of Sibyls 1 v. Mrs. Dymond 2 v.

Thomas a Kempis: The Imitation of Christ 1 v.

A. Thomas: Denis Donne 2 v. On Guard 2 v. Walter Goring 2 v. Played out 2 v. Called to Account 2 v. Only Herself 2 v. A narrow Escape 2 v.

Thomson: Poetical Works (with portrait) 1 v.

Thoth 1 v.

Trafford: *vide* Mrs. Riddell.

G. O. Trevelyan: The Life and Letters of Lord Macaulay (w. portrait) 4 v. Selections from the Writings of Lord Macaulay 2 v.

Trois-Etoiles: *vide* Murray.

Anthony Trollope: Doctor Thorne 2 v. The Bertrams 2 v. The Warden 1 v. Barchester Towers 2 v. Castle Richmond 2 v. The West Indies 1 v. Framley Parsonage 2 v. North America 3 v. Orley Farm 3 v. Rachel Ray 2 v. The Small House at Allington 3 v. Can you forgive her? 3 v. The Belton Estate 2 v. Nina Balatka 1 v. The Last Chronicle of Barset 3 v. The Claverings 2 v. Phineas Finn 3 v. He knew he was Right 3 v. The Vicar of Bullhampton 2 v. Sir Harry Hotspur of Humblethwaite 1 v. Ralph the Heir 2 v. The Golden Lion of Granpere 1 v. Australia and New Zealand 3 v. Lady Anna 2 v. Harry Heathcote of Gangoil 1 v. The Way we live now 4 v. The Prime Minister 4 v. The American Senator 3 v. South Africa 2 v. Is he Popenjoy? 3 v. An Eye for an Eye 1 v. John Caldigate 3 v. Cousin Henry 1 v. The Duke's Children 3 v. Dr. Wortle's School 1 v. Ayala's Angel 3 v. The Fixed Period 1 v. Marion Fay 2 v. Kept in the Dark 1 v. Frau Frohmann, etc. 1 v. Alice Dugdale, etc. 1 v. La Mère Bauche, etc. 1 v. The Mistletoe Bough, etc. 1 v. An Autobiography 1 v. An Old Man's Love 1 v.

T. Adolphus Trollope: The Garstangs of Garstang Grange 2 v. A Siren 2 v.

Mark Twain: The Adventures of Tom Sawyer 1 v. The Innocents Abroad; or, the New Pilgrims' Progress 2 v. A Tramp Abroad 2 v. "Roughing it" 1 v. The Innocents at Home 1 v. The Prince and the Pauper 2 v. The Stolen White Elephant, etc. 1 v. Life on the Mississippi 2 v. Sketches 1 v. Huckleberry Finn 2 v. Selections from American Humour 1 v.

The Two Cosmos 1 v.

"Vèra," Author of— Vèra 1 v. The Hôtel du Petit St. Jean 1 v. Blue Roses 2 v. Within Sound of the Sea 2 v. The Maritime Alps and their Seaboard 2 v. Ninette 1 v.

Victoria R. I.: *vide* Leaves.

Virginia 1 v.

L. B. Walford: Mr. Smith 2 v. Pauline 2 v.   Cousins 2 v.   Troublesome Daughters 2 v.

Lew. Wallace: Ben-Hur 2 v.

M. Wallace: Russia 3 v.

Eliot Warburton: The Crescent and the Cross 2 v.   Darien 2 v.

Mrs. Humphry Ward: Robert Elsmere 3 v.

S. Warren: Passages from the Diary of a late Physician 2 v.   Ten Thousand a-Year 3 v.   Now and Then 1 v.   The Lily and the Bee 1 v.

"Waterdale Neighbours," Author of— *vide* Justin M{c}Carthy.

Miss Wetherell: The wide, wide World 1 v.   Queechy 2 v.   The Hills of the Shatemuc 2 v.   Say and Seal 2 v.   The Old Helmet 2 v.

.. ᵗʰim and its Consequences 1 v.

W⸱ ⸱ite: Holidays in Tyrol 1 v.

R. Whiteing: The Island 1 v.

"Who Breaks—Pays," Author of— *vide* Mrs. Jenkin.

J. S. Winter: Regimental Legends 1 v

H. F. Wood: The Passenger from Scotland Yard 1 v.

Mrs. Henry Wood: East Lynne 3 v.   The Channings 2 v.   Mrs. Halliburton's Troubles 2 v.   Verner's Pride 3 v.   The Shadow of Ashlydyat 3 v.   Trevlyn Hold 2 v.   Lord Oakburn's Daughters 2 v.   Oswald Cray 2 v.   Mildred Arkell 2 v.   St. Martin's Eve 2 v.   Elster's Folly 2 v.   Lady Adelaide s Oath 2 v.   Orville College 1 v.   A Life's Secret 1 v.   The Red Court Farm 2 v.   Anne Hereford 2 v.   Roland Yorke 2 v.   George Canterbury's Will 2 v.   Bessy Rane 2 v.   Dene Hollow 2 v.   The Foggy Night at Offord, etc. 1 v.

Within the Maze 2 v.   The Master of Greylands 2 v.   Johnny Ludlow (*First Series*) 2 v.   Told in the Twilight 2 v.   Adam Grainger 1 v.   Edina 2 v.   Pomeroy Abbey 2 v.   Lost in the Post, etc. By Johnny Ludlow 1 v.   A Tale of Sin, etc. By Johnny Ludlow 1 v.   Anne, etc. By Johnny Ludlow 1 v.   Court Netherleigh 2 v.   The Mystery of Jessy Page, etc. By Johnny Ludlow 1 v.   Helen Whitney's Wedding, etc. By Johnny Ludlow 1 v.   The Story of Dorothy Grape, etc. By Johnny Ludlow 1 v.

Margaret L. Woods: A Village Tragedy 1 v.

Wordsworth: Select Poetical Works 2 v.

Lasceiles Wraxall: Wild Oats 1 v.

Edm. Yates: Land at Last 2 v.   Broken to Harness 2 v.   The Forlorn Hope 2 v.   Black Sheep 2 v.   The Rock Ahead 2 v.   Wrecked in Port 2 v.   Dr. Wainwright's Patient 2 v.   Nobody's Fortune 2 v.   Castaway 2 v.   A Waiting Race 2 v.   The Yellow Flag 2 v.   The Impending Sword 2 v.   Two, by Tricks 1 v.   A Silent Witness 2 v.   Recollections and Experiences 2 v.

Miss Yonge: The Heir of Redclyffe 2 v.   Heartsease 2 v.   The Daisy Chain 2 v.   Dynevor Terrace 2 v.   Hopes and Fears 2 v.   The Young Step-Mother 2 v.   The Trial 2 v.   The Clever Woman of the Family 2 v.   The Dove in the Eagle's Nest 2 v.   The Danvers Papers, etc. 1 v.   The Chaplet of Pearls 2 v.   The two Guardians 1 v.   The Caged Lion 2 v.   The Pillars of the House 5 v.   Lady Hester 1 v.   My Young Alcides 2 v.   The Three Brides 2 v.   Womankind 2 v.   Magnum Bonum 2 v.   Love and Life 1 v.   Unknown to History 2 v.   Stray Pearls (w. port.) 2 v.   The Armourer's Prentices 2 v.   The two Sides of the Shield 2 v.   Nuttie's Father 2 v.

The price of each volume is 1 *Mark* 60 *Pfennig.*

Neues Handbuch der *Englischen* Conversationssprache von A. *Schlessing.*   bound ℳ 2,25.

A new Manual of the *German* Language of Conversation by A. *Schlessing.*   bound ℳ 2,25.

Collection of German Authors.

B. Auerbach: On the Heights, 3 v. Brigitta, 1 v. Spinoza, 2 v.

G. Ebers: An Egyptian Princess, 2 v. Uarda, 2 v. Homo Sum, 2 v. The Sisters, 2 v.

Fouqué: Undine, Sintram, etc., 1 v.

Ferdinand Freiligrath: Poems, 1 v.

W. Görlach: Prince Bismarck, 1 v.

Goethe: Faust, 1 v. Wilhelm Meister's Apprenticeship, 2 v.

K. Gutzkow: Through Night to Light, 1 v.

F. W. Hackländer: Behind the Counter [Handel und Wandel], 1 v.

W. Hauff: Three Tales, 1 v.

P. Heyse: L'Arrabiata, etc., 1 v. The Dead Lake, etc., 1 v. Barbarossa, etc., 1 v.

Wilhelmine von Hillern: The Vulture Maiden [die Geier-Wally], 1 v. The Hour will come, 2 v.

S. Kohn: Gabriel, 1 v.

G. E. Lessing: Nathan the Wise and Emilia Galotti, 1 v.

Fanny Lewald: Stella, 2 v.

E. Marlitt: The Princess of the Moor [das Haideprinzesschen], 2 v.

Maria Nathusius: Joachim von Kamern and Diary of a poor young Lady, 1 v.

Fritz Reuter: In the Year '13, 1 v. An old Story of my Farming Days [Ut mine Stromtid], 3 v.

Jean Paul Friedr. Richter: Flower, Fruit and Thorn Pieces, 2 v.

J. V. Scheffel: Ekkehard. A Tale of the tenth Century, 2 v.

G. Taylor: Klytia, 2 v.

H. Zschokke: The Princess of Brunswick-Wolfenbüttel, etc., 1 v.

Series for the Young.

Lady Barker: Stories About, 1 v.

Louisa Charlesworth: Ministering Children, 1 v.

Mrs. Craik (Miss Mulock): Our Year, 1 v. Three Tales for Boys, 1 v. Three Tales for Girls, 1 v.

Miss G. M. Craik: Cousin Trix, 1 v.

Maria Edgeworth: Moral Tales, 1 v. Popular Tales, 2 v.

Bridget & Julia Kavanagh: The Pearl Fountain, 1 v.

Charles and Mary Lamb: Tales from Shakspeare, 1 v.

Emma Marshall: Rex and Regina, 1 v.

Captain Marryat: Masterman Ready, 1 v.

Florence Montgomery: The Town-Crier; to which is added: The Children with the Indian-Rubber Ball, 1 v.

Ruth and her Friends. A Story for Girls, 1 v.

Mrs. Henry Wood: William Allair, 1 v.

Miss Yonge: Kenneth; or, the Rear-Guard of the Grand Army, 1 v. The Little Duke. Ben Sylvester's Word, 1 v. The Stokesley Secret, 1 v. Countess Kate, 1 v. A Book of Golden Deeds, 2 v. Friarswood Post-Office, 1 v. Henrietta's Wish, 1 v. Kings of England, 1 v. The Lances of Lynwood; the Pigeon Pie, 1 v. P's and Q's, 1 v. Aunt Charlotte's Stories of English History, 1 v. Bye-Words, 1 v. Lads and Lasses of Langley; Sowing and Sewing, 1 v.

The price of each volume is 1 *Mark* 60 *Pfennig.*

Tauchnitz Dictionaries.

A complete Dictionary of the English and German languages for general use. By *W. James*. Thirtieth Stereotype Edition. crown 8vo sewed Mark 4,50.

A complete Dictionary of the English and French languages for general use. By *W. James* and *A. Molé*. Thirteenth Stereotype Edition. crown 8vo sewed Mark 6,00.

A complete Dictionary of the English and Italian languages for general use. By *W. James* and *Gius. Grassi*. Tenth Stereotype Edition. crown 8vo sewed Mark 5,00.

A New Pocket Dictionary of the English and German languages. By *J. E. Wessely*. Sixteenth Stereotype Edition. 16mo sewed Mark 1,50. bound Mark 2,25.

A New Pocket Dictionary of the English and French languages. By *J. E. Wessely*. Fifteenth Stereotype Edition. 16mo sewed Mark 1,50. bound Mark 2,25.

A New Pocket Dictionary of the English and Italian languages. By *J. E. Wessely*. Twelfth Stereotype Edition. 16mo sewed Mark 1,50. bound Mark 2,25.

A New Pocket Dictionary of the English and Spanish languages. By *J. E. Wessely* and *A. Gironés*. Twelfth Stereotype Edition. 16mo sewed Mark 1,50. bound Mark 2,25.

A New Pocket Dictionary of the French and German languages. By *J. E. Wessely*. Fourth Stereotype Edition. 16mo sewed Mark 1,50. bound Mark 2,25.

A New Pocket Dictionary of the Italian and German languages. By *G. Locella*. Third Stereotype Edition. 16mo sewed Mark 1,50. bound Mark 2,25.

A New Dictionary of the Latin and English languages. Seventh Stereot. Ed. 16mo sewed Mark 1,50. bound Mark 2,25.

A New Pocket Dictionary of the French and Spanish languages. By *L. Tolhausen*. Stereotype Edition. 16mo sewed Mark 1,50. bound Mark 2,25.

Technological Dictionary in the French, English and German languages by *A.* and *L. Tolhausen*. Complete in three Parts, crown 8vo sewed Mark 26,50. Each Part separately: *French, German, English* [Third Edition, with a grand Supplement] Mark 9,50. (Grand Supplement separate Mark 1,50.) *English, German, French* [Third Edition, with a grand Supplement] Mark 9,00. (Grand Supplement separate Mark 1,00.) *German, English, French* [Second Edition] Mark 8,00.

A Hebrew and Chaldee Lexicon to the Old Testament. By Dr. *Julius Fürst*. Fifth Edition. Translated from the German by *Samuel Davidson*. Royal 8vo sewed Mark 19,00.

No orders of private purchasers are executed by the publisher.

BERNHARD TAUCHNITZ, LEIPZIG.